THE DIPLOMATIC VOICE

GUIDE TO MULTILATERAL DIPLOMATIC COMMUNICATION

WISNIQUE PANIER, PhD

COLLECTION OF CREDIA

COMMON GROUND

First published in 2025
as part of the **The Global Studies Book Imprint**

Common Ground Research Networks
University of Illinois Research Park
2001 South First St, Suite 201 L
Champaign, IL 61820 USA

Library of Congress Cataloging-in-Publication Data Forthcoming

Cover Design: Copyright @ Phillip Kalantzis-Cope

Cover Image: Image Copyright

DISCLOSURE

This book is a product of the work of the Centre for Research and Expertise in Diplomacy and Artificial Intelligence (CREDIA). It is part of a series of publications initiated by the latter. It is a personal work of the author, Winique Panier. The opinions and views expressed in this book are his own and do not necessarily reflect those of the Ministry of Foreign Affairs of Haiti, the Permanent Mission of Haiti to the United Nations, or any other governmental institution or international organization mentioned or not. It is intended to provide perspectives and strategies on diplomatic communication in a multilateral context, based on his personal experiences and research. It should not be interpreted as a statement of official Haitian or international policies.

5.1.   Time Management   101

5.2.   Management of Stage Fright   102

5.3.   Use of Visual Aids   102

5.4.   Interaction with the Audience   103

5.5.   Mastery of Nonverbal Communication   103

        5.5.1.   Gestures and Body Language   103

        5.5.2.   Appropriate Dress   104

        5.5.3.   Throughput and Clarity   105

        5.5.4.   Breathing Techniques   105

        5.5.5.   Eye Contact   106

        5.5.6.   Managing Emotions   106

5.6.   Continuous Evaluation and Improvement   107

        5.6.1.   Strengths and Weaknesses to Be Considered   107

                 5.6.1.1.   Strengths to Be Identified and Enhanced   107

                 5.6.1.2.   Mastery of Files or Technical Expertise   108

                 5.6.1.3.   Diplomatic Language   108

                 5.6.1.4.   Ability to Build Alliances   109

                 5.6.1.5.   Conflict Management   111

                 5.6.1.6.   Persuasive Communication   112

                 5.6.1.7.   Networks and Relationships   114

        5.6.2.   Weaknesses to Be Identified and Improved   115

                 5.6.2.1.   Self-assessment   118

                 5.6.2.2.   Seeking Feedback   118

                 5.6.2.3.   Formation Continue   118

                 5.6.2.4.   Adapting to Changes in the Diplomatic
                            Landscape   118

                 5.6.2.5.   Conclusion and Additional Resources   119

5.7.   Some Good Practices for Multilateral Meetings   120

        5.7.1.   Careful Preparation   120

        5.7.2.   Active Listening   120

LIST OF ABBREVIATIONS

ASEAN—Association of Southeast Asian Nations
AU—African Union
BBNJ—Biodiversity Beyond National Jurisdiction
COP21—Paris Climate Conference
EU—European Union
ILC—International Law Commission
NATO—North Atlantic Treaty Organization
NGOs—Non-governmental organizations
OAS—Organization of American States
UNEP—United Nations Environment Programme
UNFCCC—United Nations Framework Convention on Climate Change
UN—United Nations
WHO—World Health Organization
WTO—World Trade Organization

LIST OF FIGURES

The images illustrating the content of this book were produced by the author himself during his participation in various multilateral meetings. They constitute real scenes of multilateral meetings that testify to his experience and his active involvement in international diplomatic forums. These photographs offer an authentic glimpse into the context of the discussions and negotiations presented in this book.

LIST OF TABLES

FOREWORD

It is with great pride and honor that I present *The Diplomatic Voice*, a remarkable book written by Wisnique Panier. This book is much more than just a compendium of diplomatic communication techniques. Above all, it is a practical guide and a true compass for all those who venture into the rich and deep world of multilateral diplomacy.

With more than forty years of experience in diplomacy, including as minister of foreign affairs and Permanent Representative of Haiti to the United Nations (UN), I have had the opportunity to work alongside many talented diplomats. Wisnique Panier stands out among them for his vast knowledge, his analytical capacity, his dedication to his work, his professionalism, and his great mastery of the art of written and oral communication.

For nearly four years, I have had the privilege of seeing Wisnique work at our Permanent Mission of Haiti to the UN. He has made a brilliant contribution to the work of the Sixth Committee, demonstrating a thorough mastery of international legal cases and a remarkable ability to draft and present persuasive interventions.[1] His keen sense of strategy and his understanding of multilateral dynamics have made him a key player in our negotiations.

The Diplomatic Voice is the fruit of this rich experience. Structured in seven chapters, this guide comprehensively explores the multiple aspects of speaking and speechwriting in international forums. In this book written in a clear and descriptive style, Wisnique shares with us proven techniques, in-depth analysis, and sound advice drawn from his many years of experience on the international stage.

The importance of this book lies not only in its practical content but also in its ability to marry theory and practice. It offers a clear and accessible understanding of the demands of diplomatic communication, while providing concrete tools to excel in this delicate art. This guide is a must-have for anyone engaging in diplomacy, whether they are seasoned experienced *professionals* or aspiring students.

But beyond the technical aspects, *The Diplomatic Voice* embodies a vision of diplomacy based on respect, cooperation, and commitment to the common

---

[1] Examples of Persuasive Discourse in International Negotiations: Nelson Mandela's 1994 speech at the UN helped to restore South Africa's image after the abolition of apartheid.

good. Wisnique reminds us that every intervention in international forums is an opportunity to build bridges, strengthen alliances, and contribute to a constructive dialogue between nations.

At a time when global challenges require effective international cooperation more than ever, this book is of crucial relevance and importance. It sheds light on the often-complex paths of multilateral diplomacy[2] and gives its readers the tools to excel at it.

I am convinced that *The Diplomatic Voice* will be a source of inspiration and a valuable guide for all those who aspire to play an active and effective role in international affairs. Wisnique Panier offers us here a reference work, which will undoubtedly mark diplomatic literature.

I invite you to immerse yourself in the pages of *The Diplomatic Voice*, an indispensable guide that not only illuminates the intricacies of multilateral communication but also inspires each reader to become a key player in building a more harmonious and effective diplomatic world. Read it and let yourself be guided toward diplomatic excellence.

HE Mr. Antonio Rodrigue, Ambassador, Permanent Representative of Haiti to the UN, Former Minister of Foreign Affairs, Career Diplomat

---

[2.] Multilateral diplomacy refers to interactions between several States or international organizations within the framework of institutional forums such as the United Nations, the European Union, the African Union, or the World Trade Organization.

PREFACE

The inspiration for this book was born from my beginnings as an advisor at the Permanent Mission of Haiti to the United Nations (UN). A few days after my arrival, an enlightened colleague, First Secretary Mrs. Linouse Vilmeney, gave me a small three-page document entitled: *Guide d'interventions à l'usage des délégué haïtiens*, from the Haitian Ministry of Foreign Affairs, written by the Haitian diplomat emeritus, Fritzner Gaspard, current Deputy Permanent Representative of Haiti to the UN. This succinct document, though imbued with diplomatic wisdom, was intended to guide diplomats in the delicate art of multilateral interventions.

He started from the observation that "Haitian delegates (diplomats and/or internal officials) intervene little or almost nothing in international meetings" (2). After listing the main explanatory factors of this reality, this guide hilghlights the consequences of the lack of intervention by Haitian delegates, the importance of interventions and the prerequisites for the preparation of interventions.[3] The clarity and relevance of Gaspard's advice was an invaluable source of guidance for me in my first speeches at the Sixth Committee of the UN General Assembly.

This little guide was much more than just a reference; it was an intellectual catalyst that sparked in me the desire to dig deeper into the intricacies of multilateral diplomacy. The need for a more exhaustive and contemporary resource became apparent, and so began the intellectual journey that led to the writing of *The Diplomatic Voice*.[4] This book is a natural extension of Fritzner Gaspard's legacy, an attempt to provide modern diplomatic actors, international relations students, and professors with a comprehensive guide, rooted in the complex reality of multilateral meetings.

The enlightening influence of the little guide in question was not the only source of inspiration in the development of *The Diplomatic Voice*. The Permanent Representative of Haiti to the UN, Ambassador Antonio Rodrigue, has also

---

[3] *Importance of Diplomacy Preparation*: A diplomat should always anticipate potential questions and criticisms to answer them confidently and consistently.

[4] The word "diplomacy" comes from the Greek *diplōma*, meaning "document folded in half," used in Roman times to refer to passports and official credentials.

played a key role in the development of this intellectual enterprise. His diplomatic wisdom, enriching experiences and unwavering commitment to excellence have been a constant inspiration.

In addition, my interactions with experienced colleagues such as Willy Louis, Minister Counsellor; Guy Métayer, former Deputy Permanent Representative of Haiti to the UN; and other colleagues such as Christopher Pierre, Betor Guensy, and many colleagues from the Sixth Committee of the UN General Assembly have contributed significantly to the evolution of this initiative. The fruitful exchanges, the enlightened advice, and the wealth of experience shared by these seasoned diplomats have nourished the very substance of *The Diplomatic Voice*. This book, thus, stands as a synthesis of multiple influences to offer a complete and up-to-date diplomatic manual.

As we embark on this journey through the intricacies and complexities of multilateral meetings, it is essential to remember that every statement, every speech delivered in these diplomatic forums has profound meaning and can influence the course of world history. This guide aspires to be a compass for those navigating these diplomatic waters, offering practical advice, in-depth analysis, and solutions to address the unique challenges faced by actors engaged in multilateral diplomacy. Multilateral meetings are not simply arenas where diplomats give speeches. They are forums where nations interact, ideas intertwine, and crucial agreements are forged. Every word[5] spoken can be a catalyst for change, every gesture can strengthen or weaken international relations. Understanding the nuance of speeches, the dynamics of statements, and the art of diplomatic communication[6] is the key to thriving in this complex environment.

The exploration of this guide leads us through the different forms of speaking, from memorable speeches to informal interventions.[7] He guides us through the careful preparation of statements, emphasizing the importance of clarity, consistency, and relevance. In addition, it details presentation techniques, highlighting the impact of nonverbal communication and skillful time management. But this guide goes beyond practical advice. It looks at the complex challenges that diplomatic actors can face, from language barriers to differences of opinion. It offers pragmatic solutions, encouraging dialogue, the search for compromise, and

---

[5.] "Words have more power than weapons."—Napoleon Bonaparte.

[6.] Diplomatic communication is a set of techniques and strategies used by States and organizations to express official positions and negotiate on the international stage.

[7.] An informal statement can be a behind-the-scenes discussion between heads of state, like the exchanges between John F. Kennedy and Nikita Khrushchev during the Cuban Missile Crisis, which led to a de-escalation.

perseverance in the search for common solutions. The study of the functioning of the UN General Assembly in this guide offers a window into the central arena of multilateral meetings, emphasizing the importance of procedure, coordination, and careful preparation.

In conclusion, this guide is more than a manual. It is a living resource, a companion for those who engage in multilateral diplomacy. It celebrates the importance of effective communication in building lasting international relationships and offers valuable tools for those looking to excel in this delicate art. May every reader find in this book useful advice, inspiring ideas, and a source of inspiration to contribute to a world where multilateral diplomacy is a vector of progress, peace, and mutual understanding.

ACKNOWLEDGMENTS

The realization of this work would never have been possible without the collaboration and participation of countless people. First, I would like to express my deep gratitude to the Great Architect of the Universe, who guided me and gave me the intelligence to carry out this work.

I also want to express my deep gratitude to my parents and family, whose love, unconditional support, and encouragement have been a constant source of strength throughout this intellectual journey. Without their presence at my side, the realization of this work would not have been possible. To them, I dedicate this work with all my gratitude and affection.

I would like to express my sincere thanks to the former Permanent Representative of the Mission, His Excellency (HE) Mr. Antonio Rodrigue, and to the Deputy Permanent Representative, Mr. Fritzner Gaspard. Their unwavering support, constant encouragement, and careful proofreading of the entire manuscript have greatly contributed to the enrichment of this work. I would also like to express my gratitude to Mr. Pierre Éricq Pierre, the New Permanent Representative of Haiti to the United Nations, for his support and trust at a pivotal stage of this project. Their long and fruitful experience in Haitian diplomacy has been a valuable source of inspiration. I express my gratitude to the Haitian minister of foreign affairs, HE Mr. Jean-Victor Harvel Jean Baptiste, for his support.

I would like to express my deep gratitude to all my colleagues at the Permanent Mission of Haiti to the United Nations (UN), particularly Betor Guensy, Enock Faustin, Joussie Montilmé, Wislyne Pierre, WIlly Louis, Bernadette Salomon, Miousemine Celestin, Wanaima Latortue and Christopher Pierre, whose collaboration was invaluable throughout the drafting process of this book. A special tribute to my collaborator, Mrs. Carline Deryce (Mrs. Der), without whom the Mission would be almost dysfunctional.

I thank the former Minister of Foreign Affairs and former Prime Minister Dr. Claude Joseph, chairman of the EDE Party's Strategic Council, for his valuable advice.

I would also like to thank the UN Library Service for its invaluable assistance in providing access to the documentation and virtual resources essential to the production of this book.

I would also like to express my deepest thanks to the director of UNITAR, Ambassador Marco Suazo, who believed in this project from the outset and actively supported it.

I would like to express my gratitude to the experts from various committees of the UN General Assembly as well as to the delegates who have come from their respective capitals to participate in various events, including the process of negotiating the conventions. Their sharing of experiences and perceptions was of great value for the development of this book. Some generously took the time to proofread our manuscript and give us their wise advice.

Many of these experts and delegates provided me with relevant information, on condition of anonymity, about the working practices within their delegations. Out of respect for their privacy, their names are not mentioned here.

I would like to thank especially some personalities who took the time to read and comment on the manuscript. My special thanks go to my friend Pierre Michelot Jean Claude; the Haitian minister of foreign affairs, HE Dominique Dupuy; her chief of staff and friend Ricarson Dorce; the Haitian Ambassador to Canada HE Mr. Arthus Weibert; and the Chargé d'Affaires ad interim of Haiti in Paris HE Mr. Louino Volcy.

Finally, I would like to thank the experts in public communication whose valuable advice has enabled me to better understand the communication issues of multilateral diplomacy. I am thinking of Professor Jean Charron, researcher and full professor at Université Laval; Professor Jean-Claude Chery; as well as my friends and collaborators Michelot Jean-Claude and Pares Jérôme.

To all of you, I extend my sincere thanks for your support and invaluable contributions to this book.

DEDICATION

To my extended family members, including my parents and siblings. To my wife Suze Delorier and my children Witshelle, Maira, and Léo for their unwavering love, invaluable support, and constant encouragement. To my colleagues at the MPH, for their frank collaboration and professionalism. To all those who, by their faith in me, have made this dream possible.

With all my gratitude and affection.

INTRODUCTION

In a world where every word can shape history and every gesture can transform international relations, multilateral diplomacy presents itself as an arena where the precision of speech is a formidable weapon.[1]

Welcome to the world of *The Diplomatic Voice*, an ultimate guide to mastering the art of drafting and presenting effective statements at multilateral meetings. Whether you are a seasoned diplomat, a political representative, a civil society actor, or a professional aspiring to participate in international discussions, this guide will provide you with the essential tools to make your voice heard with impact and influence in multilateral meetings. Should we emphasize that "multilateral diplomacy consists in the set of international procedures by which the States of a region and beyond settle their common interests and their differences through agreements in which each commits itself to several others" (Mauritius 2002, 175).

Indeed, multilateral meetings involve the participation of several countries or stakeholders to discuss, negotiate, and cooperate on issues of common interest. They are available in various formats such as international summits, conferences, diplomatic negotiations,[2] consortia meetings, and general assemblies of international organizations. These forums foster dialogue, collaboration, and collective decision-making to solve complex global problems (Revel 2011).

In the mysteries of global diplomacy, multilateral meetings are emerging as crucial platforms where links between nations are forged, and where the major decisions that shape our world are forged. These forums, often the scene of speeches and declarations, represent much more than ceremonial moments. They are points of intersection between history, politics, and diplomatic communication.[3]

[1.] *A State that is well prepared in terms of communication is more likely to influence international debates and promote its interests.*

[2.] A good diplomat must master the art of persuasive argumentation, based on concrete facts and historical or legal references.

[3.] We strongly recommend that you read the book, *How to Plan and Conduct Model U.N. Meetings: A Handbook for Organizers*. It is a practical guide that offers detailed guidance and guidance for planning and conducting UN modeling meetings. It provides essential information on how to organize these meetings effectively, with a focus on logistics, debate management, voting procedures and negotiation skills. The book aims to help organizers create realistic and informative simulations of the UN, thus promoting participants' learning about global issues, diplomacy and international relations. In summary, it is a valuable resource for those who wish to orchestrate Model United Nations in an effective and educational manner (UN Office of Public Information 1961).

This guide, the result of an in-depth exploration of the intricacies and multilateral encounters, plunges the reader into a world where every word spoken carries the weight of international responsibility. Considering the importance of speaking through the lens of chairing sessions, he focuses on the delicate art of formulating speeches, writing impactful statements, and presenting them with unparalleled mastery.

Before we venture into the practical details, it is essential to understand why multilateral meetings essential pivots in global diplomacy. They represent unique opportunities for nations to present their positions, influence debates, and build crucial alliances. The statements at these meetings are not simply speeches but powerful instruments for expressing beliefs, influencing policies, and strengthening diplomatic ties.

In response to the following question: "What is a key moment when you managed to influence an important decision in a multilateral negotiation?" a twenty-seven-year diplomat replied in this way:

> A defining moment for us was during the negotiations on the Paris Climate Agreement. We have worked closely with other countries to promote ambitious targets for emissions reductions and the transition to renewable energy. Through our active diplomacy and persuasive efforts, we helped forge a historic agreement that was widely hailed as a crucial step forward in the fight against climate change.

The essence of the declarations in these forums goes far beyond the mere expression of national positions. These speeches have a variety of purposes, from public diplomacy to building alliances, to responding to international concerns and preparing the ground for future negotiations. Each is a complex piece in the puzzle of international relations, shaping the perception of nations and influencing global dynamics.

This practical and comprehensive guide will guide you through each step of the process of drafting and presenting statements at multilateral meetings.[4] You'll learn how to structure your speeches, choose the appropriate tone, use compelling arguments, and captivate the audience's attention. Whether you need to present a political position, defend a national policy, or negotiate international agreements, this guide will be your trusted companion.

This book explores the different forms of reading mediums, from prepared speeches to visual presentations to the use of the teleprompter, highlighting the benefits and best practices of each approach. You will also discover tips for

---

[4.] *Speechwriting as a Strategic Tool: Winston Churchill said that "words are the only thing that lasts forever." His speech "We Shall Fight on the Beaches" (1940) remains a model of diplomatic and military persuasion.*

interacting effectively with your colleagues, creating professional connections, and facilitating cooperation in multilateral meetings.

Whether you aspire to influence global policy, defend human rights, promote peace, or solve humanitarian crises, *The Diplomatic Voice* will provide you with concrete advice to help you achieve your goals. You will learn how to communicate clearly, use diplomatic language, adapt your speech to different audiences, and successfully navigate the complex world of diplomacy.

The methodological framework for the drafting of this guide is based on a diverse base. We have drawn on our years of diplomatic experience at the United Nations (UN), our careful observation, our twenty years of professional practice, and our scientific research in the field of public communication. The major goal is to provide readers with a practical guide that transcends pure theory to prepare them effectively for the complex challenges of international diplomacy.

Our methodology, rooted in this perspective, followed a rigorous sequence to ensure the credibility and relevance of this book. We conducted an in-depth contextual analysis, examining historical developments,[5] current geopolitical issues, and emerging trends in multilateral relations. This understanding of the global context allowed us to address the specificities of speechwriting in this complex framework.

We then conducted a comprehensive literature review, exploring a multitude of sources ranging from official documents from the UN and other multilateral organizations to relevant academic work and iconic speeches delivered at multilateral meetings. The UN Virtual Library has been very useful to us. This documentary research was complemented by the consultation of internationally renowned experts, particularly in the field of public communication, diplomacy, and international relations. Their perspectives and advice have enriched our understanding and approach.

The collection of empirical data was another essential pillar of our methodology. We have analyzed speeches delivered at various recent multilateral meetings in different contexts and four years of observation at the various meetings at the UN Headquarters in New York and in Vienna (Austria), Jamaica (Kingston), and other regional spaces for multilateral discussion to identify current trends in speechwriting and presentation.

Based on the data collected and our personal expertise in multilateral diplomatic communication, we developed solid conceptual frameworks to structure the book.

[5.] The earliest forms of multilateral diplomacy can be traced back to the European Congresses of the nineteenth century, including the Congress of Vienna (1815), which was intended to ensure stability after the Napoleonic Wars.

These frameworks helped define key areas to be explored, including narrative structure, geopolitical issues, persuasion strategies, quiet diplomacy, and more.

Collaborative writing was a fundamental aspect of our approach, involving researchers and public communication professionals. This collaboration ensured a diversity of perspectives and expertise. Subsequently, a crucial step in our methodology was the rigorous review of the content by peers and experts in public communication, diplomacy, and international relations, thus ensuring the accuracy and relevance of our work.

Throughout the book, we have incorporated practical examples of speeches and presentations from real-life multilateral meetings. These examples illustrate theoretical concepts and offer concrete models to readers.

Finally, we have ensured that our book remains adapted to the current developments in the field of international relations and public communication. We encourage readers to stay informed of recent developments to enrich their understanding.

Our methodology is based on an interdisciplinary approach, combining diplomatic experience, academic research, and expertise in public communication.[6] We are confident that this book will serve as a valuable resource for diplomats, students, researchers, and all those who wish to successfully navigate the complex world of multilateral meetings.

This book is made up of seven chapters. In Chapter 1, we will explore an introduction to multilateral meetings, highlighting the importance of these events and the objectives of the declarations made there. Chapter 2 will delve into the different types of multilateral meetings, including high-level meetings, with relevant examples. Then, Chapter 3 will analyze in depth the forms of speeches, ranging from diplomatic speeches[7] to declarations of principle, including mini-debates.

To prepare your statements effectively, Chapter 4 will look at essential techniques, such as setting clear goals, gathering information, and structuring your speech in a clear and coherent way. In Chapter 5, we will focus on techniques for presenting your statements, covering time management, nonverbal communication, and many other aspects. Chapter 6 will explore common challenges encountered in multilateral meetings, such as differences of opinion, language and cultural barriers, and strained diplomatic relations. We will provide you with solutions to manage these complex situations.

[6.] As Henry Kissinger said: "Diplomacy is the art of limiting power to communication." A good command of diplomatic communication allows a country to increase its influence without resorting to force.

[7.] A diplomatic speech is a strategic tool for formalizing a position, influencing international public opinion, and mobilizing support.

Finally, in Chapter 7, we will dive into the workings of the UN General Assembly, detailing the procedures for debate, the role of the Main Committees, and best practices for delivering statements at these crucial sessions. Stay with us for an informative journey through the mysteries of speaking in multilateral fora and discover how to make your voice heard effectively and persuasively. Get ready to hone your communication skills, hone your diplomatic pen, and rise to the rank of leader in multilateral meetings.

Whether you are about to make your first intervention or looking to improve your impact, *The Diplomatic Voice* will be your essential guide to impactful statements, concrete results, and guaranteed diplomatic success. Ready to make your voice heard with confidence and conviction? So, dive into the pages of this guide and get ready to stand out at the most important multilateral meetings.

CHAPTER 1

Introduction to Multilateral Meetings

This chapter presents an introduction to multilateral meetings. To this end, we will explore the origins and importance of these meetings and delve into the objectives of the declarations at these international events. This introduction allows you to understand the very essence of multilateral meetings. It lays the foundation for an effective and relevant approach to the drafting and presentation of diplomatic statements.[1]

1.1. The Origins of Multilateral Meetings

The origins of multilateral meetings can be traced back to various key moments in world history when the need to solve common problems and foster cooperation among nations led to the creation of forums for dialogue. An early example is the Westphalia Conference in 1648, which ended the Thirty Years' War and established the modern nation-state system in Europe (Lévy 1984).[2] This historic turning point marked the recognition of the need for multilateral negotiations to reach lasting agreements between several parties. In the field of multilateral economic diplomacy, Claude Revel (2011) This states that form of diplomacy has taken on a "truly new dimension with the development of globalization" (23).

During the twentieth century, multilateral meetings gained importance with the creation of the League of Nations after World War I in 1919 and later with the UN after World War II in 1945. These organizations were founded on the belief that international cooperation was essential to maintaining peace and resolving global conflicts. Since then, other multilateral forums have emerged, such as

---

[1] In 1919, the Treaty of Versailles contained terms deemed too humiliating for Germany, contributing to the rise of resentment that led to World War II.

[2] Historically, ambassadors were considered emissaries of the sovereign. One of the first structured diplomatic networks was set up by the Byzantine Empire to spy on and influence neighboring nations.

the G7, the G20, and various specialized conferences addressing issues such as trade, environment, and human rights (Fleury and Soutou 2005).

The first significant speech at these first multilateral meetings could be attributed to U.S. President Harry S. Truman. In 1947, Truman delivered a speech to the U.S. Congress in which he laid out U.S. foreign policy, highlighting the principles that would guide U.S. international engagement, including support for nations seeking freedom and democracy.

The origins of multilateral meetings are, therefore, rooted in the recognition of the benefits of international cooperation in resolving shared problems. This historical evolution[3] continues to influence the way nations approach global issues, highlighting the continued relevance and necessity of multilateral meetings in the contemporary diplomatic landscape.

Multilateral cooperation has been a key element of global diplomacy since those early initiatives. Multilateral meetings have evolved over time to include a range of topics from international security to environmental protection, reflecting the increasing complexity of global issues.

Important milestones include the creation of the World Trade Organization (WTO) in 1995, which established a framework for multilateral trade nego-tiations, and the United Nations Framework Convention on Climate Change (UNFCCC) in 1992, which established a mechanism for cooperation to address global climate challenges.

It should be noted that the Permanent Representations to the UN and all inter-national or regional organizations such as the African Union, the OAS belong to multilateral diplomacy. In his doctoral thesis, Mérimée-Dufourcq (1995), shows that the Permanent Missions to the European Union "have particularities in terms of their composition and role. They are both representative of their State of origin and their members participate through the various bodies of the European Union in decision-making" (19). The author emphasizes that "the role of the permanent representations as a traditional diplomatic mission is essentially focused on informing the capitals and the repercussions of national education in the decision-making process of the European Union" (20).

These efforts demonstrate how multilateral meetings have continued to evolve to meet the evolving needs of the international community. The institutions created over time have helped shape the current diplomatic landscape, demonstrating the continued importance of cooperation and dialogue among nations in addressing global challenges.

[3.] The Treaty of Westphalia (1648) is often considered the starting point of modern diplomacy, introducing the principle of State sovereignty and institutionalizing negotiation between nations.

Image Taken in the Lobby of the United Nations General
Assembly in New York

1.2. Importance of Multilateral Meetings

Multilateral meetings, such as summits, the General Assembly of the UN, and other
international organizations, conferences, and meetings between diplomatic representatives of different countries, are important forums for discussing international

Photo Taken at a High-Level Meeting at the Opening
of the 79th Session of the General Assembly

issues and finding solutions to global problems. Statements made by diplomatic representatives, including heads of State and/or Government, at these meetings are often very important, as they can have a significant impact on relations between countries, as well as on the policies and decisions taken by these countries.[4]

We will see that statements made by diplomatic representatives can take different forms, such as speeches, press releases, joint statements, or resolutions that **are considered a unilateral act under international law**. These statements can cover a wide range of topics, such as peace and security, human rights, international trade, the environment, and public health. Statements made at these multilateral meetings are often the result of lengthy negotiations between participating

---

[4.] It should be noted that "The UN is the only truly universal international organization that deals with issues that transcend national borders and cannot be solved individually by countries. While conflict resolution and peacekeeping continue to be among its most visible activities, the United Nations and its specialized agencies are working to improve the lives of people around the world in areas such as disaster relief, education, the promotion of women's rights, and the peaceful use of atomic energy," see the United Nations website: https://www.un.org/fr/global-issues.

countries and may be the result of compromises. These declarations can also serve as a basis for subsequent agreements between countries.

It is important to note that statements made by diplomatic representatives at multilateral meetings are not binding, unless they are a resolution passed by a decision-making body. However, these statements can influence the policies and decisions taken by the participating countries and can also influence public opinion in the countries concerned.

Ultimately, statements made at multilateral meetings are an important way for diplomatic representatives to express themselves on international issues and for participating countries to work together to find solutions to global problems. We will briefly examine the benefits and opportunities offered by these meetings, such as preventive diplomacy,[5] conflict resolution, the promotion of human rights and sustainable development.

1.3. Objectives of Declarations at Multilateral Meetings

Statements at multilateral meetings play a crucial role in communicating the positions, objectives and concerns of participating countries. They aim to achieve several important objectives for each delegation and for the international community. Here we will explore some of the fundamental objectives of the declarations at these meetings. These objectives may vary depending on the context and specific issues, but they generally include communicating national positions, advocating for interests, building coalitions, building consensus, and developing policy and concerted action. It is important to emphasize the fact that a declaration may only be intended to express the country's position on one or more issues.

Speakers and speakers in multilateral forums generally seek to achieve several effects when addressing national public opinion and the international community. However, it is essential to note that these desired effects are not always guaranteed and can vary depending on a variety of factors, including the quality of the speech, media coverage, the country's reputation, and the receptivity of the audience. Understanding these goals will allow you to formulate your statements strategically to achieve the desired outcomes. We listed some of the possible goals below without going into too much detail, but there could be many more.

[5.] *The Impact of Preventive Diplomacy*: The UN defines preventive diplomacy as "diplomatic action aimed at preventing a dispute from escalating into armed conflict." One example is the mediation in Macedonia in 2001, which avoided a civil war.

1.3.1. Presenting National Positions

The declarations allow the participating countries to present their official positions on issues of international interest, to defend the interests of the country. They provide a platform to clearly and publicly express national policies, priorities and preferences. For example, at the UN General Assembly in 2020, the President of the People's Republic of China, Xi Jinping, made a statement that highlighted China's position in favor of multilateralism, strengthening global cooperation, and combating trade protectionism.[6]

Also, leaders can use their speeches to mobilize their population around national causes. For example, French President Charles de Gaulle's speech in 1967, in which he declared "Vive le Québec libre!," sparked significant mobilization in Quebec and reinforced nationalist demands (archivesRC 2020).[7] Also, at the UN General Assembly in 2018, Iranian President Hassan Rouhani gave a speech affirming Iran's position on the nuclear deal, in response to the U.S. policy of withdrawing from the deal. "In his speech to the UN General Assembly, delivered hours after that of U.S. President Donald Trump, Rouhani said it was regrettable that international leaders were encouraging extremist, racist and xenophobic tendencies in a way that was not far removed from Nazism and trampling on international law" (Nations Unies 2018). This speech is available in audiovisual and print versions.

1.3.2. Influencing Debates

Declarations are a way for countries to actively participate in discussions and contribute to the development of collective solutions. By presenting convincing arguments and relevant information, countries can seek to influence the direction of the debates in their favor, even if the primary objective is not necessarily to directly convince another country. An illustrative example is Japanese Prime Minister Shinzo Abe's speech at the UN General Assembly in 2019, which highlighted Japan's commitment to nuclear disarmament and called for the adoption of a treaty banning nuclear weapons.[8]

---

[6] Statement by HE Mr. Xi Jinping, President of the People's Republic of China—United Nations General Assembly, 2020.

[7] The audiovisual version of this speech is also available via the following link: https://www.youtube.com/watch?v=amApwFT49JQ.

[8] Prime Minister Shinzo Abe's Statement at the High-Level Meeting on Disarmament"—Permanent Mission of Japan to the United Nations, 2019.

1.3.3. Public Diplomacy[9]

Speeches in multilateral forums can be used to promote public diplomacy and improve the country's image abroad for example, South African President Nelson Mandela used his inaugural speech in 1994 to promote reconciliation and national unity in South Africa, which also helped to improve his country's international image.

> *The intervention of a diplomat always has, in one way or another, a certain weight. If only because the name of the country is mentioned in front of many delegates. It also makes it possible to disseminate the Government's efforts at the international level. It also serves as a reference. (Gaspard 2012, 3)*

1.3.4. Building Alliances and Coalitions

Declarations can be used to identify points of convergence with other countries and to build strategic alliances. By highlighting common goals, countries can strengthen their collective influence. We can consider the case of the 2021 G20 Summit which saw the European Union (EU) and the US issue a joint statement[10] on climate issues, reaffirming their commitment to fight climate change and promote a transition to a green economy.[11]

1.3.5. Enlightening International Public Opinion

The declarations are opportunities for countries to share their perspectives with the international community. They play an important role in communicating national policies and motivations to the global public. For example, at the Conference of the Parties (COP26) in 2021, German Chancellor Angela Merkel[12] delivered

---

[9.] The concept of public diplomacy emerged during the Cold War, when the US and the USSR began to use media and culture to influence international opinion (e.g., Radio Free Europe against Soviet propaganda).

[10.] *The Joint Declaration and Its Impact*: International agreements often begin with a joint declaration expressing a commitment. For example, the Potsdam Declaration (1945) set out the conditions for Japan's surrender before the end of World War II.

[11.] "Joint Statement on Climate Ambition"—European Commission, 2021.

[12.] Angela Merkel's speech on migration policy in 2015 was a striking example of successful diplomatic communication.

a statement highlighting the importance of reducing greenhouse gas emissions and transitioning to renewable energy sources.[13]

1.3.6. Establish Credibility and Commitment

Declarations reflect a country's commitment to global issues and demonstrate its willingness to contribute to multilateral efforts. Consistent and constructive statements strengthen a country's diplomatic credibility. By presenting concrete ideas and proposals, countries seek to promote constructive solutions and contribute to solving global problems. Declarations play a role in formulating and promoting positive and innovative measures.

1.3.7. Addressing International Concerns

The declarations provide an opportunity for countries to respond to concerns or criticisms made by other participants. This helps to clarify positions, clear up misunderstandings, and provide direct explanations. Speakers can advocate for changes at the international level, such as reforms in international organizations or conflict resolution. For example, Malala Yousafzai's speech at the UN in 2013 made the case for girls' education and helped bring global attention to the issue.[14]

This speech was a landmark moment that brought global attention to the crucial issue of girls' education. Malala, then 16, gave this speech to the UN General Assembly to advocate for universal girls' education. She shared her poignant personal experience as a victim of an assassination attempt by the Taliban in Pakistan due to her commitment to girls' education (United Nations General Assembly 2013).

Malala highlighted the transformative power of education and called for global solidarity to ensure that every girl has the fundamental right to go to school. Her eloquent speech was praised for her courage and advocacy for human rights, particularly girls' rights to education. Malala's speech helped raise awareness among the public and world leaders about the importance of ensuring access to education for all girls, everywhere.

[13.] Par example, Angela Merkel urges nations to face up to climate change"—*Guardian*, 2021.

[14.] This speech is available online in audiovisual version via the following link: https://www.un.org/youthenvoy/fr/video/malala-yousafzai-devant-lassemblee-nations-unies-jeunesse/.

1.3.8. Sharing Expertise and Experience

There is no doubt that multilateral meetings provide an ideal platform for countries to share expertise, experiences, and best practices on specific issues.

> From the point of view of international law, the intervention allows us to know the practice of the State in the field of discussion. Indeed, the interventions of States are recorded in the minutes and minutes of the meetings. This process contributes to the formation of the rules of international law. (Gaspard 2012, 3)

By sharing knowledge and lessons learned, countries help strengthen mutual understanding, promote effective approaches, and catalyze international cooperation to address global challenges. This underlines the importance of know-how transfer and collaboration to achieve sustainable collective solutions.

For example, multilateral health forums, such as the World Health Organization's (WHO) World Health Assembly, allow countries to share experiences in fighting epidemics and strengthening health systems. For example, during the COVID-19 (coronavirus disease 2019) pandemic, many countries shared their approaches to crisis management, testing and vaccination, contributing to a coordinated global response.[15]

1.3.9. Setting the Stage for Negotiations

Statements made at multilateral meetings play a crucial role in preparing the ground for the formal negotiations that will take place during or after these events. Indeed, these discourses are not limited to the expression of national positions; They also serve as a strategic preamble, allowing countries to set milestones and set critical parameters for future discussions. These preliminary preparations are of paramount importance, as they affect the overall dynamics of the negotiations and can create a favorable environment for the search for common solutions.

In this perspective, declarations can address specific issues that will be submitted for discussion, set out guiding principles, or clarify national positions on sensitive subjects. These elements help to establish a solid frame of reference, thus creating a fertile ground for successful negotiations. In addition, declarations

---

[15] Reference: WHO, www.who.int.

Photo Taken During the Fifth Negotiating Session
of the Convention on Cybercrime

can also play a preventive role by anticipating potential divergences and looking for areas of convergence, which promotes constructive dialogue in subsequent negotiations.

1.3.10. Facilitate Internal Communication

Another crucial aspect of declarations at multilateral meetings is their role as a means of internal communication among governments and delegations. These speeches are not only limited to the international arena but also serve to coordinate positions and ensure consistency in the messages conveyed by a delegation.

The complexity of the issues discussed at the multilateral level requires careful coordination between the different actors of a delegation. The declarations, developed ahead of the meeting, provide a platform to clarify national objectives, priorities, and red lines. In this way, they help to align the entire delegation with a common position, strengthening the credibility and coherence of the message conveyed.

In addition, these speeches can also be used to inform the members of the delegation about developments in real time during the multilateral meeting. Effective internal communication is essential to ensure that each member of the delegation has the necessary information, thus promoting constructive and informed participation in the discussions. By facilitating coordination and coherence of messages, the declarations help to maximize the impact of interventions within the multilateral sphere.

1.3.11. Strengthening Alliances and Partnerships

Speeches can be used to strengthen international alliances and partnerships. For example, at the Munich Security Conference in 2020, French President Emmanuel Macron called for the strengthening of European defense cooperation, thus aiming to strengthen European alliances.

However, it is important to note that the desired effects are not always guaranteed, as the reception of the message depends on many factors, such as the quality of communication, the international perception of the country and the reaction of the audience. Sometimes, speeches can be controversial and provoke negative reactions, which can damage the country's image. For example, U.S. President George W. Bush's speech on Iraq at the UN in 2002 was widely criticized and had negative consequences for the international perception of the US. As Bernadette Rigal-Cellard (2003) has pointed out,

> President Bush nevertheless managed very quickly to convince the majority of Americans. This rallying behind the leader after the trauma of the attacks is understandable, and one can imagine that he would have been just as strong with any president. However, we can also think that there is an additional factor that increases tenfold the empathy of the majority of citizens at this time with George W. Bush. (153)

In short, statements at multilateral meetings are an essential diplomatic instrument for some States to try to influence, inform, and engage other States. They help shape the course of discussions, build positive international relations, and work collectively toward solutions to global challenges. Speeches in multilateral forums are powerful tools for national leaders, allowing them to communicate with their own people and the international community. However, the desired effects are not always achieved, and reactions can vary greatly depending on a variety of factors.

1.4. Presentation of the United Nations as a Multilateral Space

The UN system is one of the most important international structures, encompassing a collection of organizations, specialized agencies, and programs working collectively to promote peace, international cooperation, sustainable development, and the protection of human rights worldwide. Founded in 1945 in the aftermath of World War II, the UN was created with the goal of preventing future conflicts and fostering collaboration among nations. This guide is fully in line with the spirit and functioning of the UN multilateral space. We offer an overview of the main organs and agencies that make up the UN system[16]:

- *The General Assembly (GA)*: The GA is the principal deliberative organ of the UN, composed of representatives of all Member States. It meets annually to discuss international issues, adopt resolutions, and make recommendations.
- *The Security Council (SC)*: The SC is responsible for the maintenance of international peace and security. It is composed of fifteen members, including five permanent members (China, the US, France, the UK, and Russia) with the right of veto and ten elected for two-year terms.
- *The Secretariat*: The Secretariat is headed by the Secretary-General, currently António Guterres. It is responsible for implementing the decisions of the GA and the SC, coordinating the activities of specialized agencies, and conducting peacekeeping missions.

[16.] It should be noted that "The *Secretary-General*, the UN's Chief Administrative Officer, is the embodiment of the ideals of the United Nations and a spokesman for the peoples of the world, especially those who are poor and vulnerable."

The Secretary-General is appointed by the General Assembly for a renewable term of five years, on the recommendation of the Security Council.

The current Secretary-General, the ninth Secretary-General of the United Nations, is António Guterres. He took up his post on January 1, 2017.

On June 18, 2021, António Guterres was re-elected for a second term. In particular, it committed to continue to help the world chart a path out of the COVID-19 pandemic (Nations Unies 2024).

- *The Economic and Social Council (ECOSOC)*: ECOSOC plays a central role in promoting economic, social, and environmental development. It oversees a range of specialized organizations, funds, and program.
- *The International Court of Justice (ICJ)*: The ICJ is the principal judicial organ of the UN. It settles legal disputes between States and gives advisory opinions on legal issues requested by the GA, the SC, or ECOSOC.
- *Specialized Agencies*: Organizations like UNESCO, WHO, UNDP, UN-HCR, and many others operate in specific areas such as education, health, development, and refugees.
- *Programs and Funds*: Entities such as the World Food Programme (WFP), the United Nations Children's Fund (UNICEF), and the United Nations Development Programme (UNDP) work for specific causes.
- *Peacekeeping Missions*: The UN deploys peacekeepers to conflict zones to facilitate peace agreements, protect civilians, and support reconstruction.
- The UN system plays a crucial role in solving global problems, promoting cooperation, and providing a platform for international discussions on critical issues.

1.4.1. The United Nations as the Multilateral Space Par Excellence

The UN is a multilateral space par excellence. They have been central to the world stage since their inception in 1945. "The UN is the main global forum where countries can raise questions, discuss the most complex problems and bring a common response" (Nations Unies 2024). This organization, born of the common will of nations to save succeeding generations from the scourge of war, has quickly established itself as an essential forum for international cooperation and the peaceful resolution of conflicts. Its multilateral character is reflected in its inclusive structure, which now brings together 193 Member States that meet in various bodies and specialized agencies.

A Place for Global Dialogue: The UN provides a platform where nations from around the world can meet to discuss, deliberate, and negotiate solutions to the most complex problems that transcend national borders. Whether in the framework of the General Assembly, the Security Council, the Economic and Social Council, or other specialized bodies, this multilateral space facilitates an open and inclusive dialogue.

Global Diplomacy: The UN is also where global diplomacy takes place. Representatives of each Member State deploy their diplomatic skills to build alliances, negotiate agreements, resolve disputes, and formulate policies that will have an impact on the international stage.

Responding to Global Challenges: In the face of global challenges such as climate change, pandemics, armed conflict, and poverty, the UN is the place where international cooperation is forged. The negotiations, agreements, and initiatives that emerge from these multilateral forums are aimed at finding collective solutions to the problems that affect humanity.

Ensuring Respect for International Law: As the multilateral space par excellence, the UN is also the repository of international law. Their role includes promoting and upholding the legal norms that govern relations between States, thereby contributing to stability and justice in international affairs.

A Forum for Nations Large and Small: What distinguishes the UN as a multilateral space is its inclusiveness. The great powers and the smaller nations find themselves on an equal footing, each having a voice in the concert of nations. This apparent fairness gives each Member State the opportunity to participate actively in the construction of a just and balanced world order.

An Illustration of a Speech by the President of the Transitional Council of Haiti, HE Mr. Edgard Leblanc Fils, at the United Nations General Assembly in September 2024

In conclusion, the UN embodies the multilateral ideal by providing an arena where the nations of the world can work together to solve collective problems, promote peace and security, and work together for a better future. It is in this space that the bonds of world diplomacy are woven, and the contours of international cooperation are drawn.

1.4.2. Financing of the United Nations Operations

To better understand the issues related to interventions at the UN, we believe it is important to look at the way in which UN activities are financed. Analyzing the budget and assessments of UN member countries is a complex undertaking, but it offers interesting insights into the financial dynamics and influence of Member States in this international organization.

1.4.2.1. Financial Contribution from Member Countries

The UN operates thanks to the financial contributions of its Member States. Each country is required to contribute, called a "quota," which is determined according to its economic capacity. The US has traditionally been the largest contributor, providing the largest share of the UN's regular budget. This has important implications, as a substantial financial contribution could generally confer some influence on a Member State.

The proposed program budget for 2022–2023 of the UN amounts to US $3,176,029.5 million after recosting, representing a reduction of 2.8% compared to the appropriation for 2021. The resources requested are intended to finance the full, effective, and efficient implementation of mandates. The net decrease is due to technical adjustments, including the non-renewal of appropriations for multi-year projects and the closure of two entities. The proposed increase for new or expanded mandates includes funding for the United Nations Relief and Works Agency for Palestine Refugees,[17] of the Human Rights Council and the General Assembly. "Other changes include increases for special political missions, construction, enterprise resource planning, strengthening of the development pillar, and the conversion of temporary to permanent posts. A decrease is expected through

---

[17.] *Examples of Landmark UN Resolutions*: Resolutions that have had a major impact include Resolution 242 (1967) on the Israeli-Palestinian conflict, and Resolution 1973 (2011) which led to the military intervention in Libya.

more efficient delivery modalities, including increased use of online training and innovative work practices" (Nations Unies 2022).

Based on the above, we can infer that the draft budget for 2022 reflects an approach focused on efficiency and rationalization of expenditure. Technical adjustments show an adaptation to developments such as the closure of entities. The increases target crucial areas such as human rights, sustainable development, security of UN premises, and responding to new mandates. The transformation of temporary jobs into permanent posts indicates a desire to strengthen long-term mandates. The reductions are the result of innovative practices and adaptation to post-pandemic realities, showing the Organization's flexibility in the face of global challenges. Overall, the budget reflects a balance between value for money and the ability to respond to the varied mandates of the UN.

In analyzing the way the UN is funded, we believe that the level of financial contribution of a country can potentially influence its political weight within the UN. Major contributors, especially major contributors, tend to be listened to more carefully. Countries that significantly fund the UN budget can exert greater influence on the strategic directions, priorities, and decisions taken by the organization.

Also, emerging and developing countries, although sometimes less contributory in financial terms, are also seeking to increase their influence. Some of these countries are calling for reform of the quota system to better reflect changing global economic dynamics. The discussions, these discussions, are complex and often politically sensitive.

Second, influence depends not only on the financial contribution but also on a country's ability to build alliances and defend its interests. Many countries contribute to the UN budget, but all have an equal right to vote and participate in deliberations.

Finally, issues related to assessments and financial contributions are often debated as part of broader discussions on UN reform. Some argue for a more equitable redistribution of quotas to reflect contemporary economic realities and to ensure more equitable representation of Member States.

In conclusion, the analysis of the financial contributions of UN member countries offers insight into the power dynamics within the organization. However, it is crucial to recognize that influence is not only measured by financial capacity but also depends on diplomacy, alliances, and the ability to defend positions within the UN's complex multilateral forum.

1.4.3. Occupying Key Functions at the United Nations

The influence of key UN positions can be analyzed considering national categories and influence groups, highlighting systemic and strategic realities. This can be examined by considering various factors such as the distribution of leadership positions, regional alliances, and special national interests.[18]

Categorizing key positions at the UN by nationality can reveal power dynamics.[19] Some nations, due to their history, economic power, or geopolitical influence, may be overrepresented in leadership positions. This can be interpreted as a manifestation of the concept of "power imbalance" evoked by international relations researchers (Reith 2010).

Regional alliances, where certain groups of nations cooperate closely, can play a crucial role in decision-making at the UN. Authors such as Kenneth Waltz (2002, 2014), in the theory of structural realism, have highlighted the importance of regional alliances in international politics. Regional blocs can coordinate their positions and maximize their collective influence (Telbami 2002; Waltz 2014).

Strategic influence can also come from the defense of national interests. Individuals in key positions may be motivated by the need to further the interests of their home nation. This phenomenon is often discussed in the context of realism theory, where States are perceived as rational actors pursuing their own interests.

Choices and decisions at the UN can be influenced by a variety of strategic factors, including immediate national interests. Authors like Michael Porter have theorized about national competitiveness, suggesting that nations seek to maximize their competitive position on the world stage ("Michael Porter on Competition—Michael E. Porter, 1999," s. d.; O'Hara et al. 2014).

In conclusion, the systemic and strategic analysis of those in key positions at the UN requires a thorough understanding of national, regional and individual dynamics, thus reflecting the complexity of international relations.[20]

[18.] Reading books such as *Cultures and Organizations: Software of the Mind* by Geert Hofstede, which explores cultural differences in the organizational context, can provide relevant perspectives on how cultural diversity can shape the dynamics of the United Nations.

[19.] Joseph Nye, an American political scientist, defines "soft power" as the ability of a State to influence others without resorting to coercion, using culture, values, and diplomacy.

[20.] Reading Joseph Nye's works, especially on the concept of "soft power," can also provide insights into how influence can be exerted in a non-coercive way.

1.4.4. Meeting Rooms at United Nations Headquarters in New York

The exact number of rooms may vary depending on facilities and renovations over time. However, the UN has several meeting rooms and forums to accommodate the various organs, commissions, and committees that sit there. Meetings can take place in a variety of rooms and venues, each with its own function and importance. Here are some of the most significant rooms:

1. *The General Assembly*: The General Assembly Hall is one of the most emblematic places. It is where all UN Member States meet to discuss global issues and adopt resolutions. Each State has an assigned seat.
2. *The Security Council*: Meetings of the Security Council are held in the Security Council Chamber. It is the principal organ responsible for the maintenance of international peace and security.
3. *The Economic and Social Council (ECOSOC)*: ECOSOC meets in the ECOSOC Room. The body coordinates the economic, social, and related activities of the fifteen specialized bodies, their functional bodies, and five regional commissions.
4. *The Human Rights Council Chamber*: used for the sessions of the Human Rights Council, this room is dedicated to the promotion and protection of human rights around the world.
5. *Third Committee Room*: The Third Committee of the General Assembly focuses on social, humanitarian, and cultural issues. Its sessions take place in a specific room.
6. *The Trusteeship Council Chamber*: Used for Trusteeship Council meetings, this room is dedicated to the supervision of territories under the mandate of the UN.
7. *Program Coordinating Board Room*: This is where the Programme Coordinating Board meets to coordinate the activities of the UN specialized agencies, funds, and programs.

Each of these rooms is designed to meet the specific needs of UN bodies and committees, creating functional and symbolic spaces for international diplomacy.

1.5. Theoretical Approach

Although this book is primarily positioned as a practical guide, its development has been closely guided by solid theoretical references that underpin multilateral diplomacy. From a pragmatic perspective of multilateral diplomacy, several authors have stressed the need for a realistic and flexible approach to the complex challenges of the contemporary world. Henry Kissinger, a prominent diplomat and former US secretary of state, has often advocated pragmatic diplomacy, putting forward realpolitik to guide diplomatic actions (H. Kissinger 2014; H. A. Kissinger 1956; Schulzinger 2019).

Kissinger emphasizes the importance of understanding power relations and seeking realistic solutions to international problems. He believes that multilateral diplomacy must be based on clear national interests and a nuanced understanding of international dynamics. Security The pragmatism of the neorealist school, exemplified by the work of Kenneth Waltz and John Mearsheimer, offers a worldview in which States act in their own interests and multilateral alliances are often the result of the search for security and power.

A pragmatic approach recognizes the limits of idealism and the utopian vision of international relations. It focuses on tangible results, often achieved through compromise, astute negotiations, and a realistic understanding of the balance of power. In the complex arena of multilateral diplomacy, a pragmatic approach provides a robust framework for navigating the changing realities of the world, combining the pursuit of national goals with the need to cooperate to address global challenges.

It is therefore from this perspective that realist theory, with its emphasis on national interests and competition between States, discreetly permeates the pages of this guide (Balzacq and Ramel 2013; Fleury and Soutou 2005). Indeed, the recognition of political reality in multilateral negotiations and the need to protect national interests are essential elements of the proposed approach.

The constructivist approach also emerges, emphasizing the construction of social realities and shared norms (Lynch and Klotz 1999; Gauthier 2005; Avenier 2011). Diplomatic statements and speeches[21] are presented as powerful tools for influencing international perception and building consensus. References to previous treaties and agreements, as well as accepted international norms, reflect this constructivist dimension, emphasizing the importance of interactions and shared ideas in the diplomatic process.

On the other hand, the influence of liberal approaches can be felt through the emphasis on international cooperation, the search for common solutions, and the emphasis on the role of international institutions. Summits, conferences, and other forums are presented as mechanisms for collaboration

---

[21.] Some speeches have marked history, such as Winston Churchill's in 1946 introducing the concept of the "Iron Curtain," or John F. Kennedy's in 1963 ("Ich bin ein Berliner").

and dialogue among nations, reflecting the liberal principles that underpin multilateral diplomacy.

Thus, while this book focuses on practical advice, its theoretical foundation provides a solid foundation that informs the deep understanding of multilateral diplomatic dynamics (Ambrosetti 2009, 2013). By integrating these different theoretical approaches, we offer readers a practical guide rooted in a robust theoretical understanding of global diplomacy.

From a systems perspective (Bounding 1968; von Bertalanffy and Chabrol 1980), this book can be understood as a practical guide to navigating the complex system of multilateral diplomatic relations. Following the perspective of Michel Crozier, who has developed a strategic approach to organizations, we want to explore the power dynamics between the actors of the global diplomatic system (Crozier and Friedberg 1996, 2014; Crozier and Thoenig 1975).

The diplomatic system can be seen as an arena where national and international actors compete for the protection of their interests. In the light of the strategic approach, declarations and negotiations are instruments of power, used by each actor to shape the rules of the game and influence the direction of international relations.

Summits, conferences, and other forums then become strategic platforms where nations position their interests and develop tactics to achieve specific goals. Internal coordination, highlighted in the book, can be seen as a strategy aimed at strengthening the position of an actor on the diplomatic chessboard.

The systems approach, in this perspective, highlights the interconnectedness of actors, where the actions of one participant can have repercussions on the entire system. Power relations become a central element, with each actor seeking to maximize their influence while navigating a dynamic and sometimes unpredictable diplomatic environment.

In short, this book offers a practical guide rooted in a systemic and strategic approach to multilateral diplomacy, revealing the complex power games between the actors of the international system.

1.5.1. A Functionalist Approach

This work is also part of a functionalist approach by highlighting the essential role of multilateral meetings in the maintenance of international peace and stability. By examining the different forms of meetings, the objectives of diplomatic statements, the techniques for preparing and presenting speeches, and the challenges and solutions encountered during these meetings, this book seeks to understand how multilateral diplomacy fulfills different functions within the international community.

Adopting a functionalist perspective, this work explores how multilateral meetings contribute to different dimensions of international cooperation, such as conflict resolution, the promotion of human rights, economic and social development, and environmental protection. It highlights how these meetings enable States and international organizations to cooperate to address global challenges and coordinate their actions to achieve common goals.

In addition, this book also examines the obstacles and tensions that can arise in the context of multilateral diplomacy, while proposing solutions to overcome these challenges and strengthen international cooperation.[22] By highlighting the contributions and limitations of multilateral diplomacy, it aims to promote a better understanding of its role and importance in the contemporary international system.

---

[22] *Diplomatic Discourse and Tension Management*: Barack Obama's Cairo speech (2009) sought to ease tensions between the US and the Muslim world, emphasizing mutual respect and cooperation.

CHAPTER 2

The Different Types of Multilateral Meetings

Multilateral meetings come in several types, each with its own characteristics and objectives. Without going into too much detail, in this section we will discuss the different forms of multilateral meetings that can occur, such as UN General Assemblies, international conferences, regional summits, and thematic meetings. Each type of dating has its own characteristics, rules, and protocols,[1] and it is essential to understand them to tailor your statements accordingly. We will look at the key differences between these types of meetings and provide practical tips to effectively prepare for each one.

By understanding the importance of multilateral meetings, the objectives of declarations and the different types of meetings, you will be able to fully understand the crucial role of declarations in these diplomatic contexts. Here we give a detailed typology of some of these types of encounters, accompanied by relevant examples:

2.1. High-Level Meetings in Multilateral Forums

High-level meetings are a special category of multilateral meetings that bring together national leaders, heads of State and/or Government, and other eminent personalities to discuss issues of global importance. These meetings provide a platform for strategic discussions, high-level negotiations and crucial decision-making. Here we give a detailed exploration of some high-level meetings in the context of multilateral meetings, with relevant examples:

---

[1] *Diplomatic Protocol, a Historical Legacy*: Diplomatic protocol still follows practices codified under the Ottoman Empire and at Versailles under Louis XIV, where the hierarchy between States was scrupulously respected to avoid diplomatic tensions.

Illustration of the Types of Multilateral Meetings

2.2. Objectives and Impacts of the High-Level Meetings

High-level meetings are convened to discuss the world's most pressing challenges, exchange views on complex issues, and take concrete steps to address
these issues. These meetings aim to strengthen international cooperation,
build strategic alliances, and catalyze joint initiatives to address transnational
challenges.

High-level meetings have a significant impact on the global agenda and collective decision-making. The discussions and commitments made at these meetings
can influence national policies, stimulate international cooperation and direct
efforts toward common solutions. High-level meetings are also opportunities
for leaders to engage face-to-face, strengthen diplomatic relations, and build
strategic alliances.

In summary, high-level meetings in multilateral forums play a crucial role in
promoting global dialogue, finding solutions to global challenges, and building
a more stable and cooperative world order. By bringing together the leaders of
nations, these meetings create a platform where major issues can be addressed
directly, and collective actions can be planned for a better future.

2.2.1. Some Relevant Examples

As we have already noted, diplomacy and international relations are often marked by high-level events that bring together heads of state, world leaders, diplomats, and experts to discuss critical issues affecting the international community. These high-level conferences are essential platforms for multilateral dialogue, decision-making and international cooperation. In this subsection, we will explore some relevant examples of such conferences, highlighting their importance, objectives, and outcomes. These events play a key role in global policy formulation, conflict resolution and the promotion of global peace, security, and sustainable development.

2.2.1.1. G7 Summit

Discussions at G7 summits are also an opportunity for member countries to exchange views on important economic and trade issues. For example, the G7 addresses topics such as international trade, investment, economic growth, and job creation. In addition, these meetings often allow leaders to make joint decisions or coordinate actions on specific issues, which can have a significant impact on the global economy and international relations. In summary, the G7 summit is an important platform for dialogue and cooperation between the world's major economic powers.

2.2.1.2. United Nations General Assembly[2]

 Each year, the UN General Assembly brings together world leaders to discuss major global issues, international conflicts, and progress in implementing the Sustainable Development Goals. Speeches at this high-level meeting reflect national positions and commitments to global issues. "It is therefore also an opportunity to strengthen the values on which the Organization is founded, and to reactivate the ideals embodied in the Charter. On this occasion, moreover, requests are regularly made and reflect the concerns of the Member States" (Tchemako 2018, 2).

[2.] Given its importance and scope, we will develop a section on the United Nations General Assembly.

2.2.1.3. High-Level International Conferences

These meetings aim to reach consensus on pressing issues, such as climate change, biodiversity and other major environmental challenges. The Paris Climate Conference (COP21), for example, resulted in the Paris Agreement, a landmark international treaty aimed at combating global warming by limiting global warming to well below 2°C above pre-industrial levels, and pursuing efforts to limit warming to 1.5°C. These high-level international conferences play a crucial role in mobilizing countries around the world to address environmental challenges and ensure a sustainable future for the planet and its people.

2.2.1.4. International Conferences ·

International conferences are major gatherings where delegations of States and organizations come together to discuss specific topics of global importance. An emblematic example of this format is the Paris Climate Conference (COP21), which convened representatives of countries from all over the world. The aim of the conference was to negotiate concrete measures to combat climate change, illustrating the global scope and potential impact of these events.

International conferences provide a forum for discussion and cooperation on complex issues requiring a collective approach. They often address issues such as human rights, sustainable development, global security, and many other topics that transcend national borders. These meetings provide a platform for statements to be of particular importance, influencing debates and contributing to the formulation of concerted policies at the international level.

2.2.1.5. Regional Summits

Regional summits are strategic meetings where leaders of countries sharing the same geographical region meet to discuss issues specific to their area of influence. An eloquent example of this format is the African Union Summit, a meeting of African heads of State.

This summit is dedicated to the discussion of crucial themes such as peace, security, and development in Africa, thus underlining the importance of these meetings to promote regional cooperation and address common challenges (Smouts 1991).

Regional summits provide a privileged space for consultation and the formulation of policies adapted to the specific realities of a given region. The declarations emanating from these summits play a significant role in guiding regional decisions, thus shaping political and economic dynamics at the local level.

2.2.1.6. Thematic Conferences

Thematic conferences are gatherings focused on topics, covering a diverse range of fields such as business, health, education, and many others. An illuminating example of this type of event is the WHO World Health Conference, a gathering that attracts experts and decision-makers from around the world. Its objective is to explore and debate critical issues related to global health.

These thematic conferences are essential to deepen the understanding of the issues specific to a particular field. The statements made at these events have a direct impact on policies, norms, and resulting actions on a global scale. With a focus on specific topics, these meetings allow participants to share expert perspectives, exchange best practices, and make recommendations that shape the future of the sector.

2.2.1.7. Economic and Trade Forums

Economic and trade forums are crucial arenas where economic actors and government officials converge to discuss global economic and trade issues. These forums provide a unique platform to engage on pressing economic issues, explore opportunities for cooperation, and solve challenges that transcend national borders. An emblematic example of these meetings is the World Economic Forum, a prestigious initiative that brings together world leaders, business leaders, academic experts, and other key players to discuss the most pressing economic challenges and promote international cooperation.

In these forums, declarations play a crucial role. They allow government representatives and economic actors to present their perspectives on major economic and trade issues. These declarations are not only limited to the expression of national positions but also serve to establish partnerships, influence economic policies, and catalyze cooperation initiatives. Careful preparation of such statements is essential to ensure that they achieve their purpose in these dynamic and often complex environments.

Public View During the Negotiation of a Convention
on Cybercrime at the United Nations

The themes discussed at these forums are diverse, ranging from sustainable economic growth to technological innovation and the promotion of international trade. The diversity of topics reflects the complexity of global economic issues and underscores the importance of these meetings in fostering common understanding and collaborative solutions.

In conclusion, economic and trade forums represent crucial opportunities to shape global economic policies, promote international cooperation and catalyze concrete actions. Mastering the art of writing and presenting statements within these environments provides participants with a significant advantage in influencing debates, forging strategic partnerships, and helping to shape a more inclusive and resilient global economic landscape.

2.2.1.8. Regional Group Summits

Regional group summits are unique opportunities for countries in the same region to come together to address issues specific to their geographical context.

A significant example of these meetings is the ASEAN Summit, which brings together Southeast Asian countries to discuss economic, political, and cultural cooperation. These summits provide a unique platform to strengthen regional collaboration, address common challenges, and promote sustainable development in the region.

The declarations made at these summits are of particular importance, as they allow regional representatives to express their positions on crucial issues, forge consensus and set common strategic directions. The diversity of topics discussed at these meetings often includes economic, political, cultural, and social aspects, reflecting the complexity of the issues facing the region.

The careful preparation of declarations for these summits is of paramount importance, as they help to guide discussions, influence regional policies, and strengthen cohesion among participating countries. In addition, these declarations often serve as a basis for the formulation of concrete initiatives aimed at solving regional problems and promoting collective well-being.

By answering the question: "What is a key moment when you managed to influence an important decision during a multilateral negotiation?" A diplomat with more than twenty years of career told us:

> A key moment for us was during the negotiations on the Treaty on the Prohibition of Nuclear Weapons. We have worked with other Member States to promote a disarmament and non-proliferation approach. Through our persuasion efforts and active diplomacy, we have contributed to the adoption of a landmark treaty that strengthens global security by reducing the risks associated with nuclear weapons.

In conclusion, the summits of the regional groups are key moments to foster cooperation and understanding among the countries of the same region. The statements made at these meetings play a central role in setting the regional agenda, setting common priorities, and promoting harmony in the region. Mastering the art of drafting and presenting statements in this context helps to strengthen the influence of participants and foster fruitful regional cooperation.

2.2.1.9. Ministerial Meetings

Ministerial meetings are crucial forums where ministers from different countries come together to discuss specific issues of international importance. A prime example of these meetings is provided by the World Trade Organization (WTO)

ministerial meetings, which focus on discussing trade policies and trade agreements between nations.

These meetings provide a platform for ministers to share perspectives, resolve
differences and collaborate on joint initiatives. Statements made on these occasions
are of great importance as they serve to express countries' official positions on
key issues related to trade policy, economic relations, and other critical issues.

The careful preparation of declarations for these ministerial meetings is crucial,
as they help to influence political decisions, promote mutual understanding among
nations, and strengthen cooperation in specific areas. Ministers, as representatives of their governments, use these declarations to advance national interests,
promote mutually beneficial agreements, and contribute to the development of
policies that have a direct impact on international trade.

In conclusion, ministerial meetings are privileged moments for political leaders
to discuss and decide on crucial issues. The statements made at these meetings
play a central role in formulating international policies, solving complex problems, and promoting effective cooperation among nations. Mastering the art of
drafting and presenting statements in this context helps to strengthen the influence
of ministers and foster fruitful international relations.

2.2.1.10. Follow-Up Conferences

These conferences take stock of the implementation of decisions taken at previous meetings. For example, the Sustainable Development Goals follow-up
conferences review progress toward the global goals.

These examples illustrate the diversity of multilateral meetings, each contributing
to cooperation and global problem-solving at various levels, from local to global.
Each type of meeting has its own challenges, dynamics, and objectives, requiring
careful preparation and strategic communication to achieve positive results.

2.2.1.11. Meetings of the Security Council

The Security Council is responsible for the maintenance of international peace and
security. It consists of fifteen members, including five permanent members (China,
France, Russia, the UK, the US) with the right of veto, and ten members elected for
two-year terms. Meetings of the Security Council may take the form of informal
consultations or formal meetings and cover issues such as armed conflict, international

The Security Council Is Meeting on the Situation in Haiti

sanctions, and peacekeeping operations.[3] To better understand the negotiations taking place within the Security Council, David Ambrosetti (2013) offers an enlightening reading in his text entitled: *Diplomatic Negotiations in the Security Council*

2.2.1.12. United Nations Conference

UN conferences are specific meetings held to discuss and negotiate issues. They can be thematic, such as climate conferences (COPs) or human rights conferences, or geographical, such as conferences on specific regions of the world. Conferences can result in the adoption of declarations, resolutions, or binding agreements.

2.2.1.13. Specialized Meetings and Summits

The UN is regularly the venue for specialized meetings and summits that focus on crucial issues such as health, education, gender equality, migration, and many others. These meetings, designed to address specific challenges and explore solutions, bring together a variety of actors, including experts, government representatives, international organizations, and members of civil society.

---

[3] *Diplomatic Sanctions as a Tool of Pressure*: Economic sanctions against Iran in 2015 were a diplomatic lever to force Iran to negotiate a deal on its nuclear program.

These specialized forums play a critical role in providing a global platform where innovative ideas can be shared, best practices identified, and partnerships formed to address the complex challenges facing the world. Discussions often encompass a variety of areas, ranging from global health to women's empowerment, demonstrating the diversity of issues addressed by the UN.

The goal of these specialized meetings is to catalyze concerted global action to solve specific problems, to bring stakeholders together and to promote the implementation of concrete solutions. The resulting deliberations influence global policies, guide development agendas, and contribute to the achievement of the goals of the UN.

2.2.1.14. Meetings of Committees and Subsidiary Bodies

The UN commissions and subsidiary bodies are responsible for dealing with specific issues within their respective mandates. For example, the UN Commission on Human Rights examines human rights issues, while the Economic and Social Council (ECOSOC) oversees economic and social issues. These bodies meet regularly to discuss, debate, and make recommendations on specific issues.

2.2.1.15. Informal Meetings and Consultations

Apart from formal meetings, informal meetings and consultations are often held to facilitate negotiations and discussions among Member States. These meetings provide a more flexible and informal space to exchange ideas, find compromises, and resolve disputes.

It is important to note that this typology is not exhaustive and that other forms of meetings may also take place at the UN depending on specific circumstances and needs. Multilateral meetings provide an essential platform for dialogue, cooperation, and the resolution of global problems, thereby contributing to the promotion of international peace, stability, and sustainable development.

2.2.1.16. Speeches at Official Tributes

Ceremonies to pay tribute to deceased presidents and heads of State are solemn and highly symbolic moments in diplomatic life. These events require a particularly thoughtful and measured speech, where each word must be carefully weighed to pay a dignified and respectful tribute.

On such occasions, it is essential to remember the contribution and legacy of the deceased, highlighting his or her achievements and impact on his or her country and the international community. For example, by evoking the great deeds undertaken by the late head of State, we can highlight his efforts to promote peace, development, and international cooperation. This helps to contextualize the tribute in a broader context and show how his initiatives have benefited not only his own country but also other nations.[4]

In addition, it is important to show sensitivity and respect for the family and loved ones of the deceased. Expressing sincere condolences and acknowledging the pain of loss builds an empathetic connection with the audience and shows that you share their sadness. The words chosen must reflect the dignity and gravity of the moment, while conveying a message of hope and comfort.

In addition, speeches at official tributes must also include references to the importance of continuing the work of the deceased. Emphasizing the need to perpetuate his ideals and continue to work for the causes he championed is a lively and dynamic tribute that goes beyond the simple eulogy.

General Assembly: 91st Plenary Meeting,
75th Session—Tribute to the Memory of His Excellency (HE)
Mr. Jovenel Moïse, President of the Republic of Haiti

---

[4] This photo illustrates the General Assembly for a minute of silence during the meeting that paid tribute to the memory of Jovenel Moïse, president of the Republic of Haiti.

Two Haitian Diplomats Holding the Portrait of Their
Late President

Finally, the speaker must be aware of the impact of his or her performance not only on the audience present but also on the international audience that may follow the event through the media.[5] Thus, it is crucial to adopt an appropriate tone, use clear and respectful language, and maintain a posture and gestures that reflect the solemnity of the occasion.[6] To illustrate these points, we give you some examples of speeches in tribute to deceased presidents and heads of State:

- *Barack Obama's Speech at Nelson Mandela's Funeral*: A tribute to the struggle for freedom and human rights, placing Mandela in the context of world history.
- *Speech by François Hollande at the Funeral of Shimon Peres*: Highlighting Peres' commitment to peace and security in Israel and the world.
- *Bill Clinton's Speech at Richard Nixon's Funeral*: Recognizing Nixon's contributions to U.S. and international politics despite controversies.

---

[5] Since the end of the twentieth century, diplomatic communication has been profoundly transformed by the emergence of the media and social networks, which make exchanges more instantaneous but also more vulnerable to crises.

[6] *The Importance of Posture in Diplomacy*: A diplomat must control his or her body language: avoid crossing his or her arms (a sign of closure), maintain direct eye contact, and favor an upright posture to inspire confidence.

These examples, available online, show how world leaders are using tribute speeches to honor the deceased while inspiring and comforting those who remain. In short, speeches at official tributes are moments of great diplomatic importance. They require careful preparation, heightened sensitivity, and an ability to express emotions while conveying messages of respect, recognition, and continuity.

2.2.1.17. Side Events at Major Multilateral Events

Side events, organized on the sidelines of major multilateral events, play a crucial role in the international diplomatic landscape. These meetings provide additional platforms for discussions, allowing delegations to focus on specific topics, deepen certain topics, and strengthen bilateral and multilateral relations.

First, side events help to highlight issues that may not receive the necessary attention during plenary sessions. For example, discussion panels, workshops and forums can address topics such as human rights, the environment, drugs, or global health. These events provide a more intimate and interactive setting, allowing for a more in-depth exchange of views and a detailed exploration of issues.

Second, they provide representatives with unique networking opportunities. In a less formal setting than the formal sessions, delegates can establish personal and professional contacts with their counterparts, experts, and representatives

Side Event of the United Nations Office on Drugs and Crime (UNODC)

of non-governmental organizations. These informal interactions can often lead to fruitful collaborations and strategic partnerships.

Third, side events provide an opportunity to present initiatives, reports, and projects. For example, launches of sustainability reports, presentations of innovative projects or announcements of new coalitions can occur on the main events' sidelines. These presentations benefit from the attention of a targeted and interested audience, which can amplify the impact of the initiatives presented.

Fourth, these events provide a space for dialogue and quiet diplomacy.[7] During multilateral meetings, certain sensitive or contentious topics can be discussed more freely and confidentially in the context of side events. This allows stakeholders to negotiate and find common ground without the pressure of the media spotlight.

Finally, side events enrich the experience of participants by offering a variety of formats and themes. Conferences, exhibitions, film screenings, and round tables make it possible to address global issues from various angles and to engage a multitude of actors in the international debate.

As shown in Table 1, the typology of multilateral meetings helps distinguish between formal summits, technical working groups, and regional consultations.

Table 1: Summary of Some Types of Multilateral Meetings

Meeting Type	Goal	Frequency	Examples
High-level meetings	Addressing major global issues in the presence of heads of state	Annually or as needed	UN General Assembly, G20 Summit
Informal consultations	Discuss issues in a less formal environment	On-demand	Informal consultations of the UN Security Council
Working groups	Focused on specific tasks or topics	Periodic (as required)	Working groups of the UN Human Rights Council
Special committees	Created for a particular problem	Temporary	Committees of the International Court of Justice

---

[7.] A State can use quiet diplomacy to correct a mistake. For example, after French President Jacques Chirac's clumsy remarks on Turkey in 2005, French diplomacy has multiplied bilateral meetings to calm tensions.

In sum, side events at major multilateral events are essential to maximize opportunities for dialogue, learning, and collaboration. They complement and enrich official discussions, contributing to a more inclusive, interactive, and effective diplomacy.

2.2.1.18. Farewell Declarations by Heads of State to the United Nations

The farewell declarations of the heads of State at the UN are a key moment in international diplomacy. They mark the end of a presidential term and provide an opportunity to take stock of a leader's commitment on the world stage. These speeches, delivered at the UN General Assembly or other multilateral forums, allow heads of State to reaffirm the principles and values they have defended and to share their vision of the evolution of international relations.

These statements have both symbolic and political significance. They serve as a reminder of the actions carried out in the areas of international cooperation, peace, security, and development. They highlight the diplomatic successes of a mandate, such as participation in peace negotiations, the promotion of multilateral reforms, or the commitment to human rights and environmental agreements.

Beyond the assessment, these speeches are often imbued with emotion. Some heads of State express their attachment to the UN and their faith in multilateral diplomacy as a tool for resolving crises. Others adopted a more committed tone, warning of the dangers of nationalist withdrawal and calling on the international community to continue cooperative efforts. Depending on the political context of their departure, these speeches can be conciliatory and grateful, or more critical by denouncing the limits of the multilateral system and advocating for reforms.

Historically, some farewell declarations have left their mark on people's minds with their strength and vision. They offer an opportunity not only to recall a personal commitment to peace and dialogue but also to highlight the challenges ahead for the international community. These interventions are addressed not only to leaders at the UN but also to citizens of the world who are concerned about leaving a lasting mark on the international stage.

The example of the president of Poland at the 59th session of the UN General Assembly[8] illustrates the importance of these statements. In his speech he highlighted Poland's role in its democratic transformation and European integration, highlighting the progress made by his country on the international stage. He also

---

[8] See, for example, the address by HE Andrzej Duda, president of the Republic of Poland: https://journal.un.org/fr/new-york/meeting/officials/50f3a3ea-1b21-4291-be1d-ab93de6e13b1/2025-03-04, Tuesday, March 4, 2025 at the UN General Assembly.

President of the Republic of Poland During His Speech at the 59th
Session of the United Nations General Assembly

discussed the need to strengthen multilateralism and reform the UN to ensure
more effective and balanced global governance.

These farewell declarations are also a call for continuity. Outgoing leader
reminds other Member States and his successor of the importance of continuing
efforts to address global challenges such as international security, human rights,
and economic transformation. On a symbolic level, they are not only a summary
of a mandate but an act of transmission and recognition, expressing gratitude
and vision for the future of world diplomacy.

The intervention of the president of Poland at the 59th session of the UN
General Assembly illustrates how a leader uses his latest speech to take stock
of his actions, convey a message for the future, and reaffirm his country's commitments. This type of declaration plays a key role in consolidating diplomatic
relations and projecting a strategic vision for the future.

2.2.1.19. Meetings to Commemorate Important Dates

Meetings to commemorate important dates are an essential part of multilateral
diplomacy. They allow States and international organizations to recall significant

events in world history, to reaffirm commitments, and to strengthen cooperation on shared issues. These events can concern founding moments of the international order, major crises, political advances, or struggles for peace and human rights.

These meetings aim to preserve the collective memory, raise public awareness, and recall the principles on which international cooperation is based. They are also an opportunity to reaffirm commitments made in the past and to discuss ways to strengthen them in the present. The commemoration of the signing of the UN Charter, International Human Rights Day, and the anniversaries of peace treaties are all examples of events where States recall their commitment to the fundamental principles of diplomacy.

The format of these meetings varies according to their scope and meaning. Some are official ceremonies during which heads of State and Government deliver speeches that put into perspective the historical significance of an event and its current repercussions. Others take the form of diplomatic meetings where discussions are held to analyze the lessons of the past and integrate them into contemporary challenges. These meetings may also be accompanied by the adoption of joint statements or resolutions aimed at strengthening cooperation on a given subject.

These events are also spaces for symbolic diplomacy, allowing certain States to demonstrate their commitment to international causes, to strengthen alliances or, in some cases, to reconcile divergent positions on sensitive subjects. When they concern past conflictual events, these moments of commemoration can be an opportunity for the States concerned to adopt a posture of recognition and dialogue, thus contributing to peace-building and conflict prevention.

The strategic importance of these meetings should not be underestimated. Beyond their symbolic charge, they influence the dynamics of international relations and provide a platform to reaffirm fundamental principles or launch new initiatives. They allow States to assert their place on the international scene, to express their solidarity with collective causes, and to anchor their diplomatic action in historical continuity.

Thus, the meetings to commemorate important dates are much more than simple protocol events. They play a fundamental role in contemporary diplomacy, contributing to collective memory, consolidating multilateralism, and promoting cooperation based on shared values.

CHAPTER 3

A Typology of Forms of Speech

The forms of declarations made by diplomatic representatives to the United Nations (UN) and other multilateral forums are as diverse as they are varied. We give here some characteristics of diplomatic discourse and a typology of the different forms that declarations take in multilateral forums. But first, we give some definitional elements and characteristics of diplomatic discourse.

3.1. Diplomatic Discourse and Its Characteristics

Diplomatic discourse[1] is a particular form of oral or written communication used by diplomats and official representatives of States and international organizations to express positions, negotiate, defend national interests, and promote political objectives in an international context. It is characterized by its formal nature, its specific conventions, and its crucial role in international relations.

In his book entitled *Le discours diplomatique*, Jean-Marie Tremblay is interested in a universal type rather than specific variants such as foreign policy discourses marked by the beliefs of diplomats and statesmen of a given period and country. According to him, "diplomatic discourse as a universal type is outside of time and space. A discursive set is then presented, the specificity of which must be tried to be pierced" (Tremblay 2005, 4). Despite its importance in global decision-making, (Tremblay 2005) shows that "diplomatic discourse has a bad reputation: it is said to be banal and euphemistic, wooden language or lies" (1).

Indeed, diplomatic discourse is a field of research in political science and linguistics that has attracted increasing interest over the years. There is a wide literature on diplomatic discourse, highlighting key themes, trends, and work in this field. In their book *Language and Diplomacy*, Kurbalija and Slavik (2001)

---

[1] Diplomatic discourse should be clear and structured, and use neutral language to avoid any risk of verbal escalation.

Public View at a Meeting of the First Committee at the
79th Session of the United Nations General Assembly

discuss the relationship between language and diplomacy, examining how diplomats use communication to achieve their goals. It also explores the challenges
related to translation and diplomatic interpretation.

Other researchers such as Donahue and Prosser (1997) analyze diplomatic
discourse in the context of international conflicts at the UN. Their book examines how speeches influence negotiations and decisions made within the UN.
In the same context, Liu et al. (2010) explore the impact of cultural factors on
diplomatic discourse. The author examines how cultural differences influence
diplomatic communication and international negotiations.[2]

Another important book to consider is *The Diplomatic Discourse* by Villar
(2006a), which explores in depth the field of diplomatic discourse in the context of
international relations. The author introduces the concept of diplomatic discourse
by emphasizing its crucial role in the interactions between States and international

---

[2] Diplomatic communication is essential for avoiding conflicts, negotiating agreements, and defending national
interests. Poor communication can create crises, as was the case in 1914 when the clumsy handling of ultimatums
between Serbia and the Austro-Hungarian Empire precipitated World War I.

organizations. She explains how language is used as a powerful tool to achieve diplomatic goals. Constanze Villar explores the basics of diplomatic discourse, including language conventions, communication norms, and diplomatic rituals. It highlights the importance of formality and diplomacy in communication between States. The author proposes methods for analyzing diplomatic discourse, highlighting how official speeches, public statements, and negotiations can be deciphered to understand the intentions of diplomatic actors. "Diplomatic speech deserves to be taken into consideration. Expressing intentions and transactions on the world stage, manifesting or circumventing power relations, it always forms meaning" (Villar 2006b, 1). Here are some essential characteristics of diplomatic discourse:

Formality and Protocol: Diplomatic speeches are usually formulated with great formality and follow strict protocols. They are often delivered at official meetings, international summits, general assemblies, or international conferences, as we mentioned earlier.

Cautious Language: Diplomatic discourse is characterized by its cautious and measured language. Diplomats choose their words carefully to avoid misunderstandings, provocations, or negative reactions. They often use word diplomacy to promote positions without direct conflict. *Diplomats often use cautious formulas to avoid overreaction. For example, in the Sino-US negotiations, the phrase "we are concerned" signifies a **strong disagreement**, without being a direct accusation.*

Representation of National Interests: Diplomatic speeches often aim to represent and defend the national interests of the State or organization they represent. This can include advocating for political, economic, environmental, or social positions.

Persuasion and Negotiation: Diplomats use their speeches to popularize their positions and visions on a given issue at the international level, and to persuade other international actors to support their proposals, policies, or resolutions.[3] Speeches are essential negotiating tools in international relations.

International Context: Diplomatic discourses consider the international context. They may often address issues of global politics, international security, human rights, sustainable development, etc.

Balance and Mutual Respect: Diplomatic discourse generally seeks to maintain a balance between defending national interests and respecting the opinions and concerns of other States. Mutual respect is a core value.

[3.] Regardless of bilateral approaches.

Quiet Diplomacy: Sometimes quiet diplomacy is preferred over public communication. Diplomats can negotiate privately or behind the scenes to resolve sensitive issues before addressing them publicly.

Protocol and Etiquette: Diplomatic speeches often follow strict protocols when it comes to the order of speakers, the length of speeches, the rules of translation and interpretation, etc.

Cultural Adaptability: Diplomats are often confronted with a variety of international audiences. They must be able to adapt their speeches to consider cultural and linguistic differences.

Impact on International Relations: Diplomatic speeches can have a significant impact on international relations. A well-worded speech can influence world public opinion, strengthen the credibility of a State or generate international alliances: one of the striking speeches remains the one given by the French Minister of Foreign Affairs Dominique De Villepin before the outbreak of the Gulf War.

Follow-Up and Response: Diplomatic speeches are often closely followed by other States and international organizations. Formal responses or counter-arguments may be made in response to a speech.

Historical Recording: Diplomatic speeches are often recorded in international archives and serve as historical documentation. They are witnesses to past international events and policies.[4]

In summary, diplomatic discourse is a central element of international diplomacy, used to communicate, negotiate, and represent national interests in a multilateral context. It plays a crucial role in resolving conflicts, promoting peace, and shaping international relations.

3.2. Press Releases

These are written statements that are intended to be disseminated to the media and the public. Press releases, in the context of multilateral meetings, even if they have no legal value, are of particular importance as essential communication tools for countries and delegates. These written statements play a crucial role in disseminating information, clarifying positions, and managing interaction with the media and the public.

---

[4] Almost all speeches delivered at the UN during plenary sessions are available online in different formats (written and audiovisual).

First of all, press releases are used to announce agreements and diplomatic advances. When a country reaches a consensus or understanding on a specific topic in a multilateral forum, it is essential to communicate it clearly and precisely. Press releases help to formalize these accomplishments and share them with the world. For example, during climate change negotiations, a country may issue a press release announcing its commitment to reduce its greenhouse gas emissions, which helps to strengthen the credibility of its actions.

In addition, press releases are an effective way to clarify a country's position on a given issue. When complex topics are debated in multilateral organizations, there can be misunderstandings or misinterpretations. In such situations, countries can use press releases to explain their views and motivations in detail. For example, during international trade negotiations, a country can issue a press release to explain its trade policy and the reasons for its decisions.

Press releases are also useful for answering questions from the media. Journalists often seek up-to-date information and official commentary on ongoing developments at multilateral meetings. Press releases provide a reliable source of official statements and relevant data. For example, during a humanitarian crisis,[5] a country may issue a press release to provide information on the aid measures it is taking and to answer questions from the media about the situation.

In summary, press releases are strategic communication tools in the context of multilateral meetings. They are used to announce agreements, clarify countries' positions, and respond to the media. Through these written statements, countries can influence global public opinion, enhance their credibility, and contribute to transparency and mutual understanding within the international community.

3.3. Agreed Statements

It is a joint statement made by several diplomatic representatives of different countries on a given subject. Joint statements are often used to express a common position or to announce agreements between participating countries. States attending international conferences apparently accept as axiomatic the obligation to comply with the rules of procedure of the conference. A State that does not wish to comply with the rules of procedure has the option of not attending the conference. From a practical point of view, a State is in an

---

[5] A prominent example is the 1917 "Zimmerman Note," a diplomatic dispatch intercepted by British intelligence, which precipitated the US entry into World War I.

intolerable situation if it chooses to attend a conference but ignores its rules of procedure.

3.4. Resolutions

Resolutions in multilateral forums have special significance as crucial legal and political instruments.[6] These declarations adopted by a decision-making body, such as a Council or a General Assembly, play a key role in decision-making and guiding the actions of participating countries.

First, most resolutions such as those of the Security Council are binding instruments. However, the resolutions of the General Assembly are not binding. Once a resolution is adopted, participating countries are required to comply with it. This means that they should implement the specific actions or measures requested by the resolution. For example, under a UN resolution on nuclear disarmament, the countries that have adopted it must take concrete action to reduce their nuclear arsenals in accordance with the provisions of the resolution.

Resolutions are also used to set political and legal directions. They often express the collective will of the participating countries on a particular issue. For example, a resolution adopted at a multilateral meeting on human rights may express collective support for specific human rights principles and standards, thereby guiding the future policies and actions of participating countries.

In addition, the resolutions have an impact on the international agenda. They help shape the priorities and issues that will be addressed at the international level. The adoption of a resolution on a particular topic can attract the attention of the international community and encourage other countries to become more engaged on the issue. For example, a resolution on climate change can help put the issue on the global agenda and mobilize resources to combat it.

In summary, resolutions are powerful tools used in multilateral meetings to make binding decisions, guide policy, and influence the international agenda. They reflect the collective will of the participating countries and play a central role in global diplomacy by shaping the actions and priorities of the international community.

[6.] UN Security Council resolutions can be binding (Chapter VII of the Charter) or symbolic. For example, Resolution 1441 (2002) paved the way for intervention in Iraq.

3.5. Unilateral Declarations[7]

These are statements made by a single diplomatic representative on a given subject. Unilateral statements are often used to express a firm position or to make important announcements.

Unilateral declarations, in the context of multilateral meetings, have a special significance. They are statements made by a single diplomatic representative, often on behalf of his or her country, on a specific subject. These unilateral statements can be key moments during multilateral meetings, as they can express firm positions, announce important policies, or influence ongoing debates.

One of the essential characteristics of unilateral declarations is their one-person nature. Unlike other types of speeches, they are not necessarily subject to prior negotiation or consultation with other delegates. This means that the diplomatic representative who makes a unilateral declaration assumes full responsibility for its content and impact.

These statements can be used in a variety of contexts, whether to express a political position, denounce actions contrary to the interests of the country, or announce major initiatives. For example, at a multilateral meeting on international trade, a country may make a unilateral statement to announce that it will reduce its tariff barriers in a particular sector. This announcement may have a significant impact on the ongoing negotiations and prompt other countries to take similar steps.

However, it is important to note that unilateral declarations are not necessarily well received by all participants. They can sometimes create tensions or disagreements, particularly if they run counter to the interests or positions of other countries. Therefore, it is essential for the diplomat delivering such a statement to consider the potential reactions and prepare a strategy to deal with the challenges that may arise from it.

In summary, unilateral declarations are important elements of multilateral meetings, allowing a country to make its position known in a direct and uncompromising manner. They can play a significant role in shaping the debates and negotiations in these forums, but they must be used carefully to avoid unnecessary tensions and promote constructive solutions to global problems.

[7.] In 2003, the US and the UK justified their military intervention in Iraq on the basis of a unilateral declaration affirming the threat of weapons of mass destruction, without the agreement of the UN Security Council.

3.6. Informal Declarations

These are informal statements that are made in informal discussions or in informal meetings between diplomatic representatives. Informal statements can be used to gauge the views of other countries or to explore possible solutions to a given problem.

Informal statements play an essential role in multilateral meetings. Unlike formal speeches delivered at official sessions, informal statements are made in more relaxed contexts, such as informal discussions or behind-the-scenes meetings between diplomatic representatives.

One of the main features of informal statements is their non-binding and exploratory nature. They are often used to gauge the views of other countries, explore possible solutions to a complex problem, or facilitate preliminary discussions before formal negotiations. These statements allow diplomats to create a space where ideas can be exchanged more freely and potential compromises can be identified without the pressure of official discourse.

Informal declarations can be particularly useful in situations where tensions or disagreements exist between participating countries. They offer a way to defuse potential conflicts by allowing diplomatic representatives to discuss in a more open and flexible manner. In addition, they can help build trusting relationships between the parties, which is often essential for reaching mutually acceptable agreements.

For example, during negotiations on international security issues, informal statements can be used to explore potential compromises on sensitive issues such as disarmament or non-proliferation. Diplomats can meet in small, informal groups to discuss each country's views and seek creative solutions.

However, it is important to note that while informal statements may facilitate the negotiation process, they are not legally binding and do not replace formal agreements reached at formal meetings. Rather, they are a valuable complement that can help create an environment conducive to solving complex problems.

In summary, informal statements are an important tool in the toolbox of diplomats at multilateral meetings. They promote more open discussions, the search for creative solutions, and the creation of trusting relationships between participating countries, which can be essential for reaching agreements and resolving international problems.

Public View During a Break at the 28th General Assembly
of the International Seabed Authority in Jamaica

3.7. General Policy Statements

Policy statements are an essential part of multilateral meetings, as they allow participating countries to clarify their overall position on important issues. These statements serve as a compass to guide a country's foreign policy and to communicate its priorities and values to the international community.

First, policy statements are a powerful way for a country to communicate its worldview. They provide a platform to express the fundamental principles and values that guide the country's foreign policy. For example, a country may make a policy statement affirming its commitment to human rights, peace, and international cooperation, which reflects its core values.

In addition, these declarations help to define national priorities. A country can use a policy statement to highlight the issues that matter most to it on the international stage. For example, a developing country may emphasize the importance of poverty reduction and sustainable development in its policy statement, highlighting its national priorities.

Policy statements also play a role in multilateral diplomacy by helping to guide negotiations and discussions. They help define a country's initial position on a given topic and can serve as a starting point for talks. For example, in international trade negotiations, a country's policy statement may set out its objectives and red lines, making it easier for other delegations to understand.

In summary, policy statements are important tools used in multilateral forums to define a country's overall position, express its values and priorities, and guide its foreign policy. They play a key role in diplomatic communication[8] and in the formulation of national policies at the international level.

3.8. Mini-Debates: A Tradition of the ILC

Mini-debates are a well-established tradition in the International Law Commission (ILC). This Commission, an important organ of the UN, is responsible for promoting the progressive development and codification of international law. The mini-debates represent a unique method of engagement and discussion in the Commission.

A View of the Audience at the Time of a Mini-Debate of the Sixth Committee

[8.] With the emergence of artificial intelligence and digital diplomacy, diplomatic interactions could be transformed by automated negotiations and the use of real-time data.

During these mini-debates, the members of the Commission had the opportunity to discuss in depth specific issues related to international law. Unlike traditional debates, mini-debates focus on narrow and specific topics. This allows participants to delve into the details and discuss in depth the complex aspects of international law.

The mini-debates were an informal forum that encouraged the active participation of all members of the Commission. They provide a space for experts in international law to share their knowledge, views, and concerns. This promotes an open and constructive dialogue, which is essential for progress in the development of international law.

In addition, the mini-debates allowed the Commission to remain current and relevant in its work. International law is constantly evolving, and these regular discussions allow the commission to adapt to new realities and challenges.

In summary, mini-debates are an essential component of the functioning of the International Law Commission. They promoted in-depth discussion, active engagement, and the Commission's continued relevance in the field of international law. This tradition illustrates the importance of dialogue and collaboration in the development of international law.

3.9. Declarations of Principle

These are statements that set out a country's fundamental principles on a given topic. Policy statements can be used to guide a country's foreign policy and to inform other countries of its values and priorities.

They are of great importance in multilateral meetings as tools to communicate a country's fundamental principles on specific issues. They are used to state a country's values clearly and concisely, beliefs, and commitments on a given topic.

First, these declarations allow a country to publicly affirm its commitment to fundamental principles. For example, a country may issue a statement of principles on human rights, affirming its commitment to human dignity, freedom, and equality for all. This demonstrates its adherence to these universal values and strengthens its credibility on the international stage.

In addition, declarations of principle are a way to guide a country's foreign policy. They provide a frame of reference for future diplomatic decisions and actions. For example, a declaration of principles on the non-proliferation of nuclear weapons can guide a country's participation in international disarmament negotiations and treaties.

These statements also impact international relations by helping to shape the expectations of other countries. They inform other delegations of a country's values and priorities, which facilitates mutual understanding and the search for common ground. For example, a policy statement on environmental protection can help build relationships with other countries that share similar concerns.

An example of a Declaration of Principles could be the Universal Declaration of Human Rights adopted by the UN General Assembly in 1948. This declaration sets out the fundamental rights and freedoms to which all human beings are entitled, without distinction as to race, color, sex, language, religion, political or other opinion, birth, or any other status. It represents a universal commitment to human dignity and equal rights, and it guides the actions of UN Member States in the promotion and protection of human rights around the world. We can also mention the "Rio Declaration on the Environment and the Development of Forest Management Principles," adopted at the 1992 Earth Summit in Rio de Janeiro, which sets out forest management principles to promote the conservation and sustainable use of forest resources. These principles recognize the critical importance of forests to the health of the planet and the livelihoods of people, while emphasizing the need to balance the economic, social, and environmental interests associated with forest management.

In summary, declarations of principles are essential diplomatic instruments at multilateral meetings. They allow a country to express its fundamental principles, guide its foreign policy, and communicate its values to other nations. They play an important role in diplomacy by contributing to mutual understanding and the promotion of shared values at the international level.

3.10. Statements of Protest

Generally, protests are considered in international law to be unilateral acts. These are statements made to protest an action or policy of another country. Protest statements can be used to express a country's outrage and to highlight actions that it deems unacceptable.

It is a powerful diplomatic instrument used by countries to express their disagreement or dissatisfaction with an action or policy carried out by another country. They serve to publicly affirm a country's outrage and to highlight actions that it deems unacceptable on the international stage.

These declarations have several important functions. First, they allow a country to defend its interests and principles. When a country disagrees with the actions of another, it can issue a statement of protest to make its views known and protect its national interests. For example, a country may protest a violation of its borders, military aggression, or unfair trade practices.

In addition, protest statements help to raise international awareness of the ongoing issues. They draw attention to critical issues and encourage other countries to take a stand or act. For example, a statement of protest human rights violations can mobilize the international community to condemn these actions and consider sanctions.

In addition, these statements strengthen a country's diplomatic position by showing its determination to defend its values and interests. They send a clear message to other countries and can sometimes lead to negotiations to resolve the dispute. For example, a statement of protest followed by bilateral negotiations can help resolve tensions between two countries.

Nevertheless, it is important to emphasize that statements of protest can be issued at different levels, both bilaterally and multilaterally. We give a few examples to illustrate these two contexts.

Regarding the bilateral statement of protest: Two countries may issue statements of protest each other in response to actions perceived to be detrimental to the interests or values of one of the countries. A country can protest a violation of its borders by a neighboring country by issuing an official statement[9] condemning the action and calling for corrective measures. In 2012, for example, Japan issued a statement of protest South Korea after the South Korean president visited the disputed island of Dokdo (called Takeshima in Japan), which is claimed by both countries. Japan considered the visit a violation of its sovereignty and issued a strong diplomatic protest.

At the multilateral level, a group of countries may issue a declaration of collective protest a policy, action, or event that affects several countries or is contrary to internationally accepted principles. In this perspective, a group of countries can protest against a unilateral decision by a State that violates international law or jeopardizes regional peace and security. In 2014, following Russia's annexation of Crimea, several European Union member countries issued a statement of collective protest condemning this action as a flagrant violation of international

---

[9] *Differences Between an Official Statement and a Press Release*: An official statement is delivered directly by a representative of the State or organization, while a press release is a written document distributed to the media for broadcast.

law and the principles of sovereignty and territorial integrity. This statement was followed by economic and diplomatic sanctions against Russia.

These examples illustrate how protest statements can be used at different levels to express discontent and condemn actions that are perceived as unacceptable on the international stage.

These statements of protest can be made in different forms, such as official public statements, diplomatic letters, resolutions adopted at multilateral meetings, or interventions in debates in international organizations such as the UN. They are often used to express dissatisfaction, condemn actions deemed unacceptable, and call for corrective action or changes in behavior.

In summary, protest statements are an important tool of international diplomacy. They allow a country to defend its interests, raise global public awareness, and strengthen its diplomatic position. Although often used to express outrage, they can also pave the way for peaceful discussions and resolutions of international conflicts.

3.11. Statements of Support

These are statements made to express one country's support for another country's action or policy. Statements of support can be used to strengthen bilateral or multilateral relations and to express solidarity between participating countries.

Statements of support, in the context of multilateral meetings, play a crucial role in strengthening international relations and fostering collaboration among participating countries. By openly expressing their support for an action, policy, or initiative undertaken by another country, nations aim to achieve several important objectives.

A career diplomat who answered our questions told us:

> We are taking an approach based on active diplomacy and the search for compromise. We strive to understand the concerns and interests of other countries and seek solutions that can meet the needs of all. This often involves concessions on our part, but we believe it is essential to reach lasting agreements that benefit everyone.

First, they strengthen bilateral and multilateral relations. By publicly affirming their support, countries are building a strong diplomatic bond that can be beneficial for partnerships in the future. In addition, this statement of support shows solidarity between nations, demonstrating their willingness to collaborate on issues of common interest.

Significantly, statements of support are often used to promote major initiatives. This can include promoting peace and security in a conflict region, adhering to a UN resolution to resolve an international crisis, or supporting measures to combat climate change. By formally expressing their support, countries enhance the legitimacy and effectiveness of these initiatives.

Ultimately, statements of support are an essential means of diplomatic communication.[10] They allow a country to make known its position and commitment to a particular issue, while strengthening its credibility on the international stage. Through these declarations, countries establish a solid foundation for future collaboration and help promote global peace, stability, and prosperity.

3.12. Rights of Reply

At meetings at the UN and other multilateral forums, the issue of rights of reply is often a source of momentum and controversy. The right of reply allows a country or a delegation to react to statements or criticisms made by other countries during the discussions. These answers can be written or oral and are usually time-limited.

Delegations wishing to exercise their right of reply[11] may do so in a variety of ways. Sometimes, the delegates on site write and deliver the answers themselves at the meetings, which allows them to react quickly and flexibly to comments made by other participants. In other cases, the responses may be drafted by diplomats or experts in the capitals of the countries concerned and then transmitted to the delegates present to be read or delivered during the debates.

It is important to note that there are nuances in the way rights of reply are exercised. Some responses are immediate reactions to specific remarks made during the debates, while others may be prepared in advance in response to anticipated criticism or anticipated statements by other delegations. In some cases, the rights of reply can be used strategically to defend a country's

---

[10] *Diplomatic communications can be classified into three levels:*
  1. *Public Level*: Official speeches, press statements.
  2. *Confidential Level*: Diplomatic notes exchanged between ministries of foreign affairs.
  3. *Secret Level*: Discrete negotiation channels used in times of crisis (e.g., Kissinger's secret negotiations with China in 1971).

[11] *Role of Rights of Reply*: UN Member States may exercise a right of reply during sessions of the General Assembly to correct statements deemed inaccurate or offensive.

position, to refute accusations, or to counter-arguments put forward by other participants.

Prominent examples of rights of reply at the UN often include situations where countries or delegations find themselves at odds on politically sensitive or controversial issues. For example, in debates on human rights, territorial disputes or security issues, the rights of reply can be used to express differing opinions, to defend national policies or to criticize the positions of other countries.

In summary, the rights of reply to the UN are an important aspect of multilateral debates, allowing countries and delegations to respond to comments and criticisms from other participants. These replies may be written or oral and may be made by the delegates on the spot or by diplomats in the capitals of the countries concerned. Rights of reply are often used strategically to defend national positions, refute accusations, or express disagreement on important issues.

3.13. Statements by the Representatives of the Regional Groups

Representatives of regional groups play a significant role in multilateral meetings by making statements that express the positions and priorities of the member countries of their group. These declarations serve as an essential mechanism to advance the group's common interests while contributing to international dialogue. A few concrete examples of statements by representatives of regional groups illustrate how these interventions can shape discussions and outcomes in multilateral forums.

These statements are particularly important because they embody the collective voice of a specific geographic region, reflecting the convergences and divergences within the group. Representatives of regional groups are thus given a crucial responsibility for communicating and promoting common positions, which helps to strengthen regional cohesion and influence the directions of multilateral discussions. Let us take a few significant examples of statements made by representatives of regional groups during multilateral meetings.

1. *Statement by the Asia-Pacific Group of States on Climate Change (COP21)*
   - At the Paris Climate Conference (COP21), the representative of the Asia-Pacific Group of States highlighted the disproportionate impact of climate change on the region. The declaration highlighted the need for collective action to mitigate the adverse effects and called for enhanced international cooperation.

Statement by the Representative of Grenada on Behalf of the
Caribbean Community at the United Nations General Assembly

2. *Statement by the African Group on Peace and Security*
    o At the African Union Summit, the African Group issued a joint state-
      ment highlighting the challenges to peace and security on the continent.
      The statement underscored the group's willingness to work together to
      resolve regional conflicts and strengthen peacekeeping mechanisms in
      Africa.
3. *Statement from the Group of the Americas on Fair Trade*
    o At a regional economic forum, the Group of the Americas issued a
      joint statement calling for the promotion of fair trade in the region.
      Representatives discussed the need for inclusive trade policies
      and mechanisms to reduce economic disparities among member
      countries.

These examples illustrate how statements by representatives of regional groups
help shape discussions and actions at multilateral forums, while highlighting the
specific concerns of their respective regions.

3.14. Declarations of Solidarity

A speaker at a multilateral meeting may endorse a statement made by a group
to express support for that statement or to signify agreement with the positions

taken by that group. This can be done in several ways, including through public statements, votes, or joint statements.

Declarations of solidarity are a powerful diplomatic instrument used at multilateral meetings to express support and camaraderie among participating countries. They show a unity of vision, interests, or values on a specific issue or world situation. These declarations are often formulated in a way that strengthens bilateral or multilateral relations, promotes international cooperation, and highlights solidarity among countries. Statements of solidarity can take different forms and be used in different contexts. Here are some examples of situations where such statements are common:

1. *International Crises*: When a humanitarian, environmental, political, or economic crisis occurs, countries can issue statements of solidarity to express their support for the affected nations. This can take the form of promises of help, resources, or simply statements of compassion and empathy.

2. *International Conflicts*: In the context of international conflicts or geopolitical tensions, declarations of solidarity are used to affirm mutual support between allied or sympathetic countries. They can also be used to condemn actions that are perceived as aggressive or unacceptable.

3. *Multilateral Initiatives*: When a group of countries come together to promote a common cause, such as peace, sustainable development, or human rights, statements of solidarity are often developed to show their collective commitment to that cause.

4. *Joint Actions*: Statements of solidarity can accompany concrete actions or measures taken by a group of countries. For example, declarations of solidarity can be issued at the same time as economic sanctions, joint humanitarian operations, or disarmament initiatives.

5. *Global Events*: At important international events, such as international conferences, world summits, or diplomatic ceremonies, participating countries can issue statements of solidarity to highlight their common goals and commitment to international cooperation.

These declarations are often carefully crafted to reflect the common positions of the participating countries and to strengthen their unity. They can help forge strategic alliances, promote peace and stability, and increase the diplomatic influence of signatory countries.

Ultimately, declarations of solidarity are an essential diplomatic tool to promote international cooperation and mutual understanding among nations.

They are a testament to the importance of unity and solidarity in a complex and interconnected world.

3.15. Public Statement

The speaker may speak at the meeting to publicly express their support for the group's statement. For example, at a meeting on climate change, a representative of a country may say, "We wish to fully endorse the statement made by the Group of Developing Countries in support of more ambitious action to combat climate change."

3.16. Statements Before and After the Vote in Multilateral Diplomacy

Statements made before and after a vote are strategic interventions in multilateral forums. They allow States to clarify their positions, influence negotiations, and explain the reasoning behind their vote. These statements are essential in bodies such as the UN General Assembly, the Security Council, the European Union, and other international organizations where decisions are made collectively through a voting process.

Before the vote, statements aim to shape the decision-making of other States and express an official stance on the resolution under discussion. These interventions allow a country to indicate its support or reservations, reaffirm its international commitments, and suggest recommendations for potential amendments. They serve as a negotiation tool, seeking to rally support or persuade undecided members. In some cases, they are used to set conditions for a favorable vote, emphasizing the need for amendments or additional guarantees. A well-structured pre-vote statement can influence the dynamics of the debate and sway undecided members toward a particular position.

During the voting process, diplomats must adhere to the procedural rules of the organizations where they serve. Depending on the institution, the vote may be public or secret, recorded by name or conducted by a show of hands, and it may require a simple majority, a qualified majority, or unanimity. Although the actual voting process is often quick, the preceding discussions, including statements before the vote, play a decisive role in shaping the outcome.

After the vote, statements provide an opportunity for States to explain their decision and justify its implications. They may express satisfaction, reservations, or regret regarding the result of the vote. A country that has voted in favor of a resolution can reaffirm its commitment to its implementation and encourage further action. Conversely, a State that abstained or voted against may use the moment to clarify the reasons behind its decision and highlight the national principles or interests that guided its stance. A post-vote statement can also anticipate the next steps, calling for additional negotiations or suggesting adjustments in the implementation of the adopted resolution.

Post-vote statements are particularly important when a resolution is controversial or divisive. They help ease tensions, reaffirm diplomatic commitments, and prevent the vote from being perceived as a rupture in relations between certain States. When a vote is contested, these statements may also signal a country's intention to reconsider its position in the future or propose an alternative course of action.

In a diplomatic context, these statements must be carefully crafted and delivered with an appropriate tone. A pre-vote statement should be persuasive and strategic, while a post-vote statement should be balanced and diplomatically measured. In all cases, these interventions help clarify a state's position, influence international debates, and ensure consistency in diplomatic commitments within multilateral forums.

3.16.1. Choices in Voting: For, Against, Abstention, and Other Options in Multilateral Diplomacy

It is important to note that voting in multilateral diplomacy is a crucial mechanism for decision-making in international organizations, where States express their positions on resolutions, treaties, or policy recommendations. Each vote carries strategic and diplomatic significance, shaping international relations, alliances, and the global policy landscape. When participating in a vote, States typically have several options: voting in favor, voting against, abstaining, or, in some cases, choosing not to participate. Each choice reflects a country's political, legal, or strategic considerations and can have long-term implications.

Voting in Favor ("For"): When a country votes in favor of a resolution, it expresses full support for its content and objectives. This choice signifies alignment with the proposed measures and a commitment to their implementation. A "yes" vote can strengthen diplomatic partnerships, demonstrate adherence to international norms, and reinforce a state's role in shaping global policy.

A favorable vote is often preceded by negotiations and compromises to ensure the resolution aligns with national interests. States may vote in favor even if they have reservations if the resolution advances their broader diplomatic goals. A strong majority in favor of a resolution enhances its legitimacy and encourages its implementation.

Example: A country votes in favor of a UN Security Council resolution imposing sanctions on a State violating international law, signaling its commitment to maintaining global security.

Voting Against ("No"): A vote against a resolution indicates strong opposition to its content, implementation, or underlying principles. This choice may stem from political, economic, legal, or ideological disagreements. A country may reject a resolution if it believes it contradicts its national interests, infringes on sovereignty, or sets a precedent it considers harmful.

In some cases, voting against a resolution is a strategic move to signal resistance, even if the State acknowledges that the measure is likely to pass. A "no" vote can also serve as a warning against similar future initiatives.

Example: A State votes against a resolution condemning its domestic policies, arguing that the measure constitutes interference in its internal affairs.

Abstention: Abstention is a neutral stance where a State chooses not to take a definitive position on a resolution. Unlike voting against, abstention does not block the resolution, but it signals concerns, reservations, or a lack of full endorsement.

Countries abstain for various reasons, such as maintaining diplomatic balance, avoiding direct confrontation, or signaling that they are not fully convinced of the resolution's effectiveness. Abstention can also reflect internal political divisions or a desire to leave room for future negotiations.

Example: A country abstains from voting on a resolution concerning a conflict where it has diplomatic relations with both parties, seeking to maintain neutrality and preserve its mediation role.

Non-participation in the Vote: In some cases, States may choose not to participate in a vote by being absent or refraining from casting a vote. Non-participation can be a diplomatic tool to avoid taking a stance on a sensitive issue without explicitly abstaining. It can also indicate dissatisfaction with the voting process, the legitimacy of the resolution, or the procedures followed.

While non-participation does not directly impact the result of the vote, it may be interpreted as a passive form of disapproval or a reluctance to engage with the issue.

Example: A delegation walks out of a vote in protest, refusing to legitimize the discussion by participating in the decision-making process.

Veto Power (in Specific Institutions): In organizations like the UN Security Council, permanent members have the power to veto a resolution, effectively

Posting of the Results of a Vote in the United Nations
General Assembly

blocking its adoption. The veto is a stronger form of opposition than a "no" vote, as it prevents the resolution from being implemented, regardless of majority support.

Example: A permanent member of the UN Security Council vetoes a resolution on military intervention, preventing its passage despite widespread support from other members.

Strategic Considerations in Voting Choices: States carefully evaluate their voting decisions based on multiple factors:

- *Bilateral and Multilateral Relations*: Voting choices may influence diplomatic ties with allies and adversaries.
- *National Interests and Sovereignty*: A country ensures that the resolution aligns with its policies and legal framework.
- *Domestic Political Pressures*: Governments may vote in a way that reflects internal political concerns or public opinion.
- *Future Negotiations and Trade-Offs*: A State may abstain or vote against a resolution with the expectation of leveraging its position in future discussions.

3.17. Conclusion

The choices a State makes in a multilateral vote go beyond a simple yes or no decision. Each option—voting in favor, voting against, abstaining, or not participating—carries strategic weight and conveys a message to the international community. These decisions shape diplomatic engagements, define alliances, and influence global policy-making. Understanding the rationale behind voting choices is essential for navigating international relations and advancing a country's interests within multilateral frameworks.

3.18. Co-sponsorship of the Statement

Co-sponsorship of a declaration at multilateral meetings is an important diplomatic move where a country chooses to formally associate itself with the group or countries that proposed the declaration. This action reinforces the country's commitment to the declaration and demonstrates its active support for the objectives and principles expressed in the text.

When a country decides to co-sponsor a declaration, it means that it is ready to work closely with other stakeholders to promote, negotiate, and support the declaration. This approach is often used to put forward a common position or to strengthen a multilateral initiative. It can also be a means of strengthening diplomatic relations between the co-sponsoring countries. "We take a collaborative approach by seeking alliances with other like-minded countries and building coalitions to promote our common positions. We are also engaging in bilateral discussions to understand the concerns of other countries and find compromises that can be acceptable to all," said an EU diplomat.

Co-sponsorship can take various forms. For example, in the context of multilateral trade negotiations, a country may co-sponsor a joint declaration on open markets, indicating its commitment to greater trade openness. Similarly, in discussions on international security issues, several countries may co-sponsor a resolution to promote peace and stability.

This is a testament to the country's willingness to play an active and constructive role in multilateral negotiations and debates. It can strengthen the country's credibility by showing its commitment to international cooperation and promoting the creation of alliances and partnerships with other actors.

In short, the co-sponsorship of a declaration is a strategic diplomatic approach where a country formally associates itself with a declaration proposed by other countries. This reinforces the country's commitment to the objectives of the declaration and can have a significant impact on the outcome of multilateral negotiations or deliberations.

3.19. Support Through Concrete Actions

In addition to verbal statements, the stakeholder may support the statement with concrete actions, such as implementing policies or actions consistent with the statement. This demonstrates a real commitment to the principles or objectives set out in the declaration.

When a stakeholder endorses a group statement, it often reinforces the credibility and legitimacy of that statement. It can also strengthen cohesion and solidarity among the members of the group and show that they speak with one voice on the issue at hand. Ultimately, subscribing to a group statement at a multilateral meeting is an important way to strengthen cooperation and promote common positions within the international community. It would also be interesting to say that a country that is a member of a Group is not obliged to adhere to the Group's statement. An example is the Non-Aligned Group.

In summary, representatives of regional groups can make different types of statements at multilateral meetings, each with a specific purpose. These statements can be used to express the group's position on regional and international issues, to promote regional cooperation, and to express solidarity with other countries or regional groups.

3.20. Inaugural Speech

When a representative is assigned to deliver an inaugural or opening address at a conference or meeting, it is common to do so standing. This creates a solemn atmosphere and marks the importance of the event. For example, at the UN General Assembly, the opening speech is usually delivered standing by the leaders of the Member States.[12]

[12.] *The Opening Speech of the UN General Assemblies*: Brazil is historically the first country to speak at the sessions of the UN General Assembly, a tradition dating back to 1947.

The General Assembly Resumes the Fifth Session
of the Ad Hoc Committee on Cybercrime

The inaugural address occupies a special place at multilateral meetings. It marks the beginning of an important event, often with symbolic or historical significance. Here is how an inaugural address typically plays out, following a consistent structure:

1. *Greetings and Thanks*: The inaugural address usually begins with greetings and thanks. The speaker addresses the audience, the delegations present, the hosts of the event and anyone who has contributed to its organization. Thanks, are often expressed for the honor of speaking at this inaugural moment.

2. Context and Importance of the Event: The speech continues by briefly explaining the context of the event and its importance. The speaker can recall the history of the meeting, its objectives and its potential impact on the issues discussed.

3. *Vision and Goals*: A keynote address can include a section where the speaker lays out their vision for the event and the goals they hope to achieve. This

section aims to provide a general framework for future discussions and
to inspire participants.

4. *Key Themes and Topics*: The speaker can talk about the key themes and
    topics that will be discussed during the event. This helps to highlight
    priority issues and direct the audience's attention.

5. *Call to Action*: An inaugural address may include a call to action, invit-
    ing participants to fully engage in discussions, seek solutions, and work
    together to achieve positive outcomes.

6. *Historical Perspective*: In some cases, the speaker may put the event into
    perspective in relation to similar historical events or previous multilateral
    meetings. This underlines the importance of the current event.

7. *Reflection on Values and Principles*: The inaugural address may also include
    a reflection on the values and principles that will guide the discussions.
    It can serve as a reminder of the importance of diplomacy, international
    cooperation, and mutual respect.

8. *Conclusion and Encouragement*: The speech usually concludes with words
    of encouragement and optimism. The speaker can express confidence in
    the ability of the participants to address the challenges and find solutions
    to the problems discussed.

9. *Official Opening Statement*: Finally, the keynote address may end with an offi-
    cial opening statement of the event, marking the start of the planned activities.

In summary, a keynote address at a multilateral meeting is an opportunity to
set the tone and provide a conceptual framework for future discussions. It highlights the importance of the event, the objectives and the values that will guide
the exchanges. It can also inspire participants to work together constructively
to achieve meaningful results.

3.21. Foreign Policy Statement

A foreign policy statement is an official communication from a country that sets
out its position, priorities, and directions in international policy. In this section,
we provide some details on how such a statement is generally structured:

1. *Introduction and Context*: First, the foreign policy statement begins with
    an introduction that sets the context. The speaker often explains the current
    circumstances or recent developments that justify the statement.

2. *Definition of Objectives*: Next, the declaration clearly States the objectives of the country's foreign policy. This may include promoting peace, stability, human rights, fair trade, or other specific priorities.
3. *Guiding Principles*: The speaker set out the guiding principles that underpin the country's foreign policy. These principles serve as the basis for the country's decision-making and international action.
4. *Position on International Issues*: The declaration then discusses the country's specific positions on important international issues. These can be regional conflicts, global crises,[13] trade negotiations, climate change, etc. Each position is usually supported by arguments and justifications.
5. *Commitment to International Cooperation*: The declaration highlights the country's commitment to international cooperation. It can underline the importance of multilateral diplomacy, strategic alliances, or international agreements.
6. *Mention of Partners and Alliances*: The speaker may also mention international partners with whom the country works closely. This can include political, military, or economic alliances.
7. *Strategy and Action Plan*: The declaration may contain a section on the country's strategy and action plan to implement its foreign policy. This can include specific initiatives, short- and long-term goals, and priorities for action.
8. *Call to Action*: The declaration can conclude with a call to action, inviting other countries to join the country in pursuing its goals and values.
9. *Reaffirmation of National Values*: Finally, the declaration can reaffirm the country's national values, such as democracy, human rights, freedom, equality, and justice. These values are often used as the basis for foreign policy.

In short, a foreign policy statement is a key document that sets out a country's vision and priorities on the international stage. It communicates the country's position on various issues and underlines its commitment to global cooperation, while highlighting its core principles and values.

3.22. Emergency Speech

Emergency speeches are of paramount importance in multilateral meetings, as they are usually delivered in response to critical situations that require immediate

---

[13.] *Examples of Diplomatic Crises Managed by Communication*: During the Cuban Missile Crisis in 1962, secret diplomacy between the US and the USSR prevented a nuclear escalation.

action.[14] These speeches are characterized by their urgency, their potential impact on the decisions taken and their ability to quickly mobilize the participating countries.

Examples of situations where emergency speeches could be made include humanitarian crises. In the event of a major natural disaster, such as an earthquake, hurricane, or famine, an emergency speech could be made to mobilize international assistance and coordinate relief efforts.

Similarly, threats to international security may require emergency speeches. When a crisis endangers international security, such as an escalation of tensions between two countries or a major terrorist attack, an emergency speech could be made to call for immediate de-escalation or counterterrorism measures.

Global pandemics are also situations where emergency narratives are relevant. In response to a global pandemic, such as COVID-19, an emergency speech could be delivered to mobilize international resources to fight the disease, coordinate vaccination efforts, and strengthen international public health cooperation.

In addition, major environmental disasters may also require emergency speeches. In the face of an environmental disaster such as an oil spill, a chemical spill or massive deforestation, an emergency speech could be given to call for measures to protect the environment, clean up and prevent future damage.

Finally, global economic crises could also give rise to emergency speeches. In the event of a global economic crisis, such as a major recession or a collapse of financial markets, an emergency speech could be made to call for internationally coordinated economic stimulus measures and cooperation to stabilize financial markets. These examples illustrate different situations in which emergency speeches may be needed in multilateral meetings to respond to crises and mobilize immediate action by participating countries.

In these situations, it is essential that the speech is carefully prepared and delivered effectively to maximize its effectiveness. It seems important to us to specify how an emergency speech generally takes place:

1. *Quick Contextualization*: The speech usually begins with a brief contextualization of the emergency. It aims to quickly inform the hearing about the facts, issues, and consequences of the situation.
2. Call for Immediate Action: The emergency speech should contain a clear call for immediate action. This may include asking participating countries to take specific actions, mobilize resources, or support a critical initiative.

[14.] Volodymyr Zelenskyy's speech in March 2022 to the European Parliament, calling for immediate aid and Ukraine's accession to the EU, was a key moment for the mobilization of European countries.

3. *Identification of Challenges*: The discourse can also identify the main challenges that need to be faced in the context of the emergency. This can include logistical hurdles, security concerns, or political constraints.

4. Solidarity and Cooperation: Emergency speeches often emphasize the importance of solidarity and cooperation between participating countries in dealing with the situation. They insist on the need to work together to solve the problem.

5. *Resource Mobilization*: If the emergency requires specific resources, the discourse may call for the mobilization of these resources. This can be in the form of funds, personnel, equipment, or other forms of support.

6. *Firm Commitment*: Emergency speeches are characterized by a firm commitment to solving the problem. They demonstrate the commitment of the participating countries to act quickly and effectively.

7. *Coordination*: The speech can also highlight the need for effective coordination between countries, international organizations and other actors involved in the management of the situation.

8. *Support for Victims*: Depending on the nature of the emergency, the speech may express support for victims and compassion for those affected.

9. *Follow-Up*: In conclusion, the speech can refer to the need for regular monitoring of the situation and an evaluation of the actions taken.

Overall, emergency speeches are powerful diplomatic instruments that mobilize the attention and action of participating countries in critical situations. They are designed to be direct, impactful, and results-oriented. Their effectiveness depends on careful preparation, clear communication, and the ability to elicit an immediate and coordinated response.

3.23. Important Negotiations

During important negotiations or sensitive discussions, standing statements emerge as a strategic tool to emphasize the importance of the topics discussed and to consolidate the authority of the representative engaged in the talks. This approach is particularly meaningful, helping to create a serious atmosphere that reflects the seriousness of the issues discussed and to enhance the impact of the statements made.

The action of standing up to speak, often accompanied by assertive gestures, conveys a strong message. It indicates that the moment is solemn, that the issues under discussion are of crucial importance, and that the representative expressing the statement has significant authority on the subject. This intentional approach helps to capture the attention of participants and create a climate conducive to in-depth and meaningful exchanges.

In addition, standing statements are often perceived as markers of commitment and determination. They strengthen the credibility of the representative by demonstrating his or her personal investment in the topics discussed. This assertive posture can positively influence the dynamics of the negotiations by reinforcing the conviction of the other participants as to the sincerity and importance of the words spoken.

In summary, during important negotiations, the strategic use of standing statements represents a powerful tactic to raise the level of attention, emphasize the seriousness of the topics discussed, and strengthen the representative's authority. This deliberate choice of communication helps to forge an environment conducive to constructive discussions and to strengthen the impact of the statements, thus promoting the voice toward meaningful results.

3.24. Domestic Policy Statements

Domestic policy statements are official communications in which a representative announces major changes or reforms at the national level. These statements may relate to various areas, such as political reforms, economic measures, or significant social initiatives. The standing posture during these statements is often used to emphasize the seriousness and importance of the changes announced.

A notable example of a domestic policy statement is the speech of the president of the US during his annual State of the Union address. In this speech, the president updates Congress and the American people on the country's progress and announces policy priorities for the coming year. These statements are usually delivered standing before an assembly of members of Congress, Cabinet members, diplomats, and other dignitaries, and are widely broadcast on television and the internet.

Another example concerns the declarations of European leaders at European Union summits. At these meetings, EU Member States' leaders meet to discuss the most pressing political, economic, and social issues. On this

A Representation of the General Assembly During
an Intervention in the Context of a Plenary Session

occasion, heads of State or Government can make standing statements to present their country's positions on the topics on the agenda and announce important national policies.

In the context of the UN, heads of State and Government often deliver speeches at the Annual General Assembly to outline their countries' priorities and ongoing national initiatives. These speeches can also include announcements of important domestic policies, such as legislative reforms or economic and social development programs.

In summary, domestic policy statements are important tools for informing the public about the actions and directions of the national government. Standing during these statements often reinforces their importance and seriousness, making them particularly effective in communicating key messages to citizens and the international community.

3.25. Memorable Speeches at the United Nations: Marks of Length and Impact

In multilateral forums such as the UN, some speeches delivered by representatives of member countries have often made history by their length and impact. The **Guinness Book of World Records** documents statements that not only lasted several hours but also left a lasting imprint on the history of international debates.

In 1957, V. K. Krishna Menon, the representative of India, set a record by delivering the longest statement to the Security Council. His speech was spread over three meetings held on January 23 and 24, 1957, totaling more than eight hours of cumulative speaking time (S/PV.762, S/PV.763, and S/PV.764).

However, V. K. Krishna Menon was not the only speaker to take center stage with lengthy speeches. The document entitled "List of Speeches and Visits by Heads of State and Other Personalities," covering the period from 1945 to 1976, provides fascinating details about the longest statements and the personalities who made them.

Among these memorable moments was an impressive speech by Fidel Castro, leader of Cuba, at the 872nd plenary meeting of the General Assembly on September 26, 1960. His speech lasted no less than 269 minutes (A/PV.872), captivating the audience with the depth of his ideas and the passion of his delivery.

Other notable statements are also recorded in this historic document. Mr. Sékou Touré, President of Guinea, delivered a 144-minute speech at the 896th plenary meeting on October 10, 1960 (A/PV.896). Nikita Sergeyevich Khrushchev, then chairman of the Council of Ministers of the Soviet Union, also made an impression with a 140-minute speech at the 869th plenary meeting on September 23, 1960 (A/PV.869). Mr. Sukarno, then president of Indonesia, added his voice to the list with a 121-minute statement delivered at the 880th plenary meeting on September 30, 1960 (A/PV.880).

Even in the modern era, protracted speeches continue to influence discussions in the General Assembly. In 2009, Colonel Muammar Al-Gaddafi, leader of the Libyan Arab Jamahiriya, captivated the audience for ninety-six minutes at the 64th session of the General Assembly (A/64/PV.3).

These examples illustrate how speeches at the UN have the power to capture the world's attention and shape debates on issues of global importance, whether through their exceptional length, impactful content, or both. We also want to highlight several iconic speeches that have made history and had a significant impact on international diplomacy. Here are some of those memorable speeches without going into detail:

1. *John F. Kennedy's Berlin Speech (1963)*: During his visit to Berlin in the midst of the Cold War, U.S. President John F. Kennedy delivered his famous "Ich bin ein Berliner" (I am a Berliner) speech. This speech expressed U.S. solidarity with West Berlin and West Germany, marking the U.S. commitment to freedom and democracy.

Table 2 provides a comparative overview of the different forms of speech used in multilateral settings, ranging from official statements to informal consultations.

Table 2: A Summary of Different Types of Speech

Summary of the Typology of Discourse Forms	Description
Diplomatic speeches	Official speeches delivered by diplomats in international forums, highlighting national positions or policies.
Press releases	Official statements issued to the media to inform the public of diplomatic decisions or events.
Joint statements	Statements made by two or more countries to show a unified position on an issue.
Resolutions	Formal expressions of opinion or intent agreed upon by a multilateral body (e.g., the UN).
Unilateral declarations	Announcements made by a single state, often setting out its position on specific issues.
Informal statements	Less formal remarks, often made during informal meetings or consultations, to gauge reactions.
Policy statements	Statements describing a country's major policies in international or multilateral contexts.
Mini-debates	Short debates that take place in informal sessions, often used to clarify positions without a formal vote.
Policy statements	Statements made to affirm a country's commitment to certain fundamental values or principles.
Statements of protest	Statements made to formally oppose actions taken by another State or entity on the international scene.
Support statements	Statements expressing support for an initiative, resolution, or position of another country.
Right of reply	Statements made in response to the speech or accusations of another delegation during a formal meeting.

Summary of the Typology of Discourse Forms	Description
Statements by regional groups	Speeches delivered on behalf of a regional coalition of countries to present a unified vision.
Statements of solidarity	Statements made to express solidarity with a country or region in crisis or conflict.
Public statements	Official public announcements aimed at an international audience, often aimed at clarifying or strengthening policies.
Vote in favor of declarations	Statements that accompany votes in favor of specific resolutions or statements in multilateral contexts.
Co-sponsorship statements	Formal support through co-sponsorship of resolutions or declarations presented in international forums.
Supporting with concrete actions	Statements supported by concrete actions or commitments on behalf of a State.
Inaugural speeches	Keynote remarks or speeches delivered at high-level events or at the beginning of an international session.
Foreign policy statements	Statements made by States describing their international political positions or future diplomatic orientations.
Emergency speech	Urgent statements made in response to a crisis or sudden global event requiring immediate action.
Key negotiations	Statements made during important negotiations to define or strengthen a country's position.
Domestic policy statements	Speeches intended to discuss internal reforms or changes, but delivered in an international forum.
Memorable speeches	Emblematic speeches delivered at the UN that have left a lasting impact on global diplomacy.

2. *Martin Luther King Jr.'s Speech at the UN (1963)*: Martin Luther King Jr. gave a memorable speech at the UN General Assembly, advocating for civil rights and racial equality. His call for justice and nonviolence had an international impact and contributed to the fight for civil rights in the US.

3. *Nelson Mandela's Speech at the UN (1990)*: After his release from prison, Nelson Mandela gave a speech at the UN, marking his commitment to reconciliation in South Africa. His call for an end to apartheid and the establishment of a multiracial society was a defining moment in South African history.

4. *Malala Yousafzai's Speech at the UN (2013)*: Malala Yousafzai, a Pakistani activist for girls' education, gave an emotional speech at the UN after surviving an assassination attempt by the Taliban. His impassioned call for education for all has brought global attention to this crucial issue.

5. *Greta Thunberg's Speech at the UN (2019)*: Swedish environmental activist Greta Thunberg gave an impassioned speech on the climate emergency at the UN Climate Action Summit. His call for immediate action to tackle climate change has inspired global protests and increased awareness of this crisis.

6. *Kofi Annan's Speech on the Responsibility to Protect* (2005): Former UN Secretary-General Kofi Annan gave a historic speech on the responsibility to protect. He stressed the responsibility of the international community to protect populations from genocide, war crimes, ethnic cleansing, and crimes against humanity.

These and other speeches illustrated the power of speech in multilateral forums to raise awareness, mobilize and influence global public opinion, and helped shape history and international diplomacy.[15]

[15.] It should be noted that the examples of memorable speeches that we illustrate in this section are available in open access, in particular in the United Nations library in audiovisual versions and texts.

CHAPTER 4

Speech Preparation Techniques

The preparation and presentation of your statement at multilateral meetings is of crucial importance to advance your country's interests and contribute meaning-fully to global discussions. This chapter walks you through the essential steps in preparing your statement, with a focus on clarity, consistency, and persuasion.

  The purpose of this chapter is to provide you with practical advice on how to structure and present your statement effectively, considering the audience, expecta-tions, and specific issues of the multilateral meeting. You'll learn how to analyze the purpose of your statement, gather relevant information,[1] structure your arguments logically and persuasively, and adopt persuasive communication techniques.

  Carefully preparing your statement is essential to maximize its impact and ensure that it contributes constructively to the discussions. By following the steps outlined in this chapter, you will be able to present your statement in a way that positively influences the deliberations and promotes your country's interests effectively. Here are the steps to follow.

4.1. Understanding the Purpose of Your Report

Before you begin the process of writing your statement for a multilateral meet-ing, it is imperative that you have a clear understanding of the goal you want to achieve. This step is critically important, as it will lay the groundwork for your speech and guide your entire preparation. To do this, weigh yourself against the following questions:

- What message do you want to convey? Clearly identify the main points you want to address in your statement. These points should be in line with your country's interests and objectives at this multilateral meeting.

---

[1] *The Impact of Information Leaks in Diplomacy*: In 2010, WikiLeaks published confidential U.S. diplomatic cables, revealing sensitive exchanges between diplomats and creating a crisis of confidence in U.S. diplomacy.

- What results do you hope to achieve? Define the concrete goals you want to achieve with your statement. These results can vary depending on the nature of the meeting, ranging from raising audience awareness of your position to building consensus on a particular issue.
- What impact do you want to have on the audience? Consider the effect you want your statement to have on meeting attendees. Do you want to persuade them to support your point of view, inform them about a specific issue, or encourage them to take concrete action?

To ensure consistency and alignment of our discourse with our country's policies and goals at the UN, we work closely with relevant policymakers and experts. We make sure that we have a clear understanding of our government's directives and priorities, and we strive to reflect them in our speeches. "We are also open to suggestions and advice from our colleagues and diplomatic allies to ensure that our speeches contribute constructively to international debates," said a diplomat who answered our questions.

Once you have a clear understanding of the purpose of your statement, it will be easier to structure your speech, choose the most relevant arguments, and communicate persuasively. This initial stage of reflection will determine the direction of the entire process of preparing your statement for a multilateral meeting.

4.2. Analysis of the Agenda and Key Topics

Analyzing the agenda and key topics is of crucial importance in preparing your statement for a multilateral meeting. Here is how you can approach this step successfully:

First, start by carefully reviewing the agenda of the multilateral meeting. This step will allow you to understand all the topics that will be discussed during the meeting. In addition, identify key topics that are particularly relevant to your country or delegation. It is essential to focus your statements on the most important and relevant points.

Moreover, look for in-depth information on the topics in question. This research will allow you to become familiar with the issues, current debates and positions of other participating countries. Therefore, this in-depth knowledge will allow you to strengthen your arguments with solid facts and anticipate possible questions and criticisms.

According to one of the participants in this study,

> the preparation of a speech for the United Nations requires an in-depth analy-
> sis of the subject, as well as taking into account the positions and interests of
> other Member States. We start with in-depth research to understand the issues
> and perspectives, and then structure our speech logically and persuasively. We
> ensure that our arguments are supported by solid facts and data, and we adapt
> our language to reach our target audience.

Moreover, consider the potential positions of other countries. It is essential
to anticipate any arguments and objections you may encounter in the meeting.
Finally, adapt your speech according to the planned agenda. Organize your statement to address topics in the established order, starting with the most important
or relevant to your delegation.

Using these logical connectors, you will be able to analyze the agenda and key
topics in a methodical and structured way, which will strengthen your preparation
for the multilateral meeting.

4.3. Understanding the Audience

Identify the countries and organizations represented, as it is essential to know
the participants in the meeting and understand their interests and prior positions
on the topics on the agenda. This will help you anticipate any questions and
concerns that may arise during the debates. Also consider cultural differences,
as multilateral meetings often attract an international audience, which means that
cultural norms, sensitivities, and communication preferences can vary widely.
Be aware of these cultural differences and adapt your speech accordingly to
avoid any misunderstandings. Additionally, identify the audience's priorities
and issues, as it is crucial to understand the issues that matter most to them.
Review the key themes of the meeting and identify common concerns that your
speech can address.

4.4. Analyze Expectations

Before you write your statement, determine what the audience hopes to hear
from you. Is it a constructive contribution to an ongoing debate, a proposal for
solutions to specific problems, or simply a presentation of your country's position

on a particular issue? Also identify pain points, as multilateral meetings are often the place for sensitive discussions and differences of opinion. Identify any potentially controversial topics or pain points that may arise, and be prepared to respond to them in a thoughtful and constructive way.

By fully understanding your audience and anticipating their expectations, you'll be able to tailor your speech in a way that builds a stronger connection with your audience and maximizes the impact of your statement. This in-depth analysis of the audience and expectations is an essential part of preparing your statement for a multilateral meeting.

4.5. Setting Clear Objectives

Setting clear goals is a fundamental step when preparing your statement for a multilateral meeting. Before you even start writing your speech, you need to have a clear vision of what you want to accomplish with your statement.

First, understand what impact you want to have on the audience. Think about how you can influence the opinions of other delegates, promote a specific proposal, or simply share important information.

If you have specific proposals to promote, make sure your goals are aligned with their acceptance or adoption. Consider whether you are aiming to gain support from other delegations for these proposals or to advance them.

Sometimes, the main purpose of your statement may be to provide important information or updates on a particular topic. In this case, make sure that your message is clear and that the information is conveyed in an understandable way.

Your goal may be to raise awareness of a specific issue or to provide education on a complex topic. In this case, your statement should be informative and educational.

If your statement represents your country's official position, make sure your goals include protecting and promoting national interests. It could be to defend a policy or to protect the rights of your country.

In some situations, your goal may be to find common ground with other delegations and work toward consensus. In this case, your statement should be conciliatory and oriented toward the search for common solutions.

Once you have clearly defined your objectives, you can guide the writing of your statement in a strategic way. Every element of your speech, whether it is your arguments, examples, or recommendations, should be aligned with these goals. This will help you make your statement more effective and maximize its impact at the multilateral meeting.

4.6. Information Gathering and In-Depth Research

Gathering information and thorough research are crucial steps in preparing your statement for a multilateral meeting. Before you start writing your speech, you need to gather relevant information about the topics on the agenda. This in-depth research will allow you to strengthen your arguments with solid facts and support your positions convincingly.

To do this, start by consulting various sources of information, such as reports, studies, official documents, and statistical data. You can also search for academic works, press articles and specialized publications in the relevant field. Be sure to check the credibility of the sources you are viewing and cite all references correctly.

Do not hesitate to seek the advice of experts or specialists in the subject, if they are available. Their knowledge can provide you with valuable insights and informed perspectives on the matter.

In-depth research is not just limited to gathering information, it also involves a critical analysis of the data you have collected. Evaluate the relevance of each piece of information to your objective and arguments. Discern trends, correlations, and key elements that could strengthen your position.

Also, anticipate any questions and potential criticisms that your statement might generate. Prepare to respond in an informed manner using the information you've collected. This will allow you to be better prepared at the multilateral meeting and to defend your views in a solid way.

In summary, thorough research and information gathering are essential steps in preparing an effective statement at a multilateral meeting. They will strengthen your position, support your arguments with solid facts, and allow you to respond to questions and criticisms in an informed way.

4.7. Structure Your Declaration in a Clear and Coherent Way

The structuring of your statement in the context of a multilateral meeting is of paramount importance. A well-structured speech ensures that your message is clear, consistent, and understandable to your diverse audience. Here is how you can organize your return in a logical and fluid way.

4.7.1. Presentation of Key Points

When laying out your key points in a statement at a multi-stakeholder meeting, using logical connectors is crucial to ensure clarity and consistency in your speech. Here is how to organize your ideas logically and sequentially using these connectors:

First, identify the key points you want to address in your statement. These items should be relevant to the agenda of the multilateral meeting and your specific objectives.

Then, organize your ideas logically using logical connectors. For example, you can start by saying, "First, we're going to look at the impact of climate change on our ecosystems." This connector ("first") makes it clear that you are going to introduce your first key point.

In addition, continue to guide your audience through your key points using connectors such as "next" or "more." For example, you might say, "Next, let's address the impact of climate change on the global economy." These connectors signal a natural transition to the next point in your statement.

Additionally, be sure to maintain a logical sequence in the presentation of your key points. Each point you address should be articulated consistently with the previous one, creating a smooth progression in your statement.

In conclusion, the judicious use of logical connectors will allow you to present your key points in an organized and understandable way for your audience. This will enhance the impact of your statement at the multilateral meeting and make it easy for delegates to follow your speech.

4.7.2. Crafting a Catchy Introduction

A powerful introduction is essential to capture your audience's attention from the very beginning of your statement. Use anecdotes, key figures, or provocative statements to generate interest. Briefly introduce the topic and clearly state your position or goal. A strong introduction will help you connect with your audience and get them to listen carefully to your statement.

4.7.3. Development of Persuasive Arguments

Using convincing arguments is essential to persuade the audience of your position. Use relevant facts, statistics, case studies, and examples to back up your claims. Be persuasive and avoid vague generalities. Anticipate potential counter-arguments and be prepared to respond to them thoughtfully and convincingly.

By carefully preparing at each stage of your statement writing, you will be able to convey your message effectively and persuasively at multilateral meetings. In the next part of this guide, we will cover how to write your statement in detail, exploring techniques for adapting your language to diplomacy, avoiding ambiguities, and creating an eye-catching introduction.

In developing your arguments at a multilateral meeting, using logical connectors can greatly enhance the consistency and understanding of your statement. Here is how to approach this step using logical connectors:

First, identify the key points you want to address in your statement. These items should be directly related to the topics on the agenda of the multilateral meeting.

Then, for each key point, develop your arguments in detail. Present facts, statistics, and real-world examples to support your arguments. You can use logical connectors such as "for example," "in addition," or "with respect to" to introduce your examples and strengthen your arguments. For example, you might say, "When it comes to climate change, it's critical to note that global greenhouse gas emissions have increased alarmingly in recent years."

Additionally, be sure to maintain consistency in how you develop your arguments. Make sure that each point you address articulates logically with the previous one, creating a fluid thread in your statement.

Also, do not forget to relate your arguments to the interests of your delegation or country. Explain why each point is relevant to your country and how it could benefit from the position you are advocating.

In conclusion, by developing your arguments logically and using appropriate connectors, you build the credibility of your statement and allow your audience to follow your reasoning effectively. This will help make your statement more persuasive and impactful at the multilateral meeting.

4.7.4. Maintaining Consistency

Consistency in a speech is essential to ensure that ideas follow each other in a logical way and that the audience can follow the thread of the discussion without confusion. To maintain this consistency, it is important to make sure that there is a smooth transition between each idea or section of the speech. This means that you should avoid abrupt jumps from one topic to the next, making sure that each new idea flows naturally from the last. To achieve this, it is important to use logical connectors such as "in addition," "on the other hand," "therefore," and "in conclusion." These transition words will serve as guides for the audience, helping them understand how each new idea fits into the overall context of the speech. By maintaining this consistency, you ensure that your message is clear, compelling, and easy to follow for everyone listening.

4.7.5. Use of Clear and Concise Language

When writing your statement for a multilateral meeting, the use of clear and concise language is essential. In a diplomatic context, where the audience is made up of delegates from diverse cultural backgrounds and where time is usually limited, effective communication is crucial. Here is how you can ensure that your language is both clear and accessible:

To start, **use simple words**. Opt for common terms rather than complex technical expressions. Avoid using jargon that could make your speech difficult to follow for those who are not experts in your field. Simple language promotes universal understanding.

Also, **avoid excessively long sentences**. Wordy sentences can make it difficult to understand your message. Prefer short, direct sentences to convey your ideas more effectively. This allows your audience to better assimilate your words.

By using **logical connectors**, you can connect your ideas seamlessly. For example, say, "Also, let's look at the economic implications of this proposal." These connectors help your audience easily follow your reasoning and perceive the coherence of your speech.

Keep in mind that your **audience may have diverse cultural and linguistic backgrounds**. So, avoid idioms and cultural references that might not be understood by everyone. Your speech must be accessible to an international audience.

To **clarify your points**, do not hesitate to use **illustrative examples**. For example, you might say, "To illustrate this concept, let's take a concrete example from our recent experience." Examples help make your ideas more tangible and understandable.

Finally, **conciseness** is essential in diplomatic speeches, where time is of the essence. Avoid long, superfluous speeches. Every word should help reinforce your message in a precise and succinct way.

By adopting a clear and concise language approach, you increase your chances of positively influencing your audience's opinions and contributing meaningfully to multilateral discussions.

4.7.6. Adapt Your Language to Diplomacy

Diplomacy requires nuanced and polite language. When writing your statement, be sure to use appropriate diplomatic terms, avoid offensive or aggressive statements, and favor a respectful and constructive tone. Adapt your language to the audience and the nature of the multilateral meeting, keeping in mind the diplomatic protocols and norms in force. Some authors such as Arifon (2010) show the importance of diplomatic language.[2] In his article, the author offers a historical and anthropological perspective of the diplomat's forms of expression. In particular, he seeks to understand why diplomatic language is both formal and necessary: characteristics that bring it closer to wooden language (Delporte 2009).

4.7.7. Avoid Ambiguities and Misunderstandings

Clarity is key when writing your statement. Avoid ambiguous sentences, confusing formulations, or overly technical terms that could lead to confusion. Use accurate and concise language to ensure that your message is understood unequivocally, minimizing the chance of misunderstandings or misinterpretation.

In other words, to ensure effective communication in your statement, it is imperative to avoid ambiguities and misunderstandings. This means that you should strive to use clear, precise, and concise language. Avoid complex sentences that could lead to confusion, as well as technical terms that may not be understood by all delegates. "When writing speeches, we strive to be clear, concise and persuasive. We use appropriate diplomatic language and avoid overly technical or partisan terms. We also ensure that our discourse is balanced and respectful of the different perspectives represented in the General Assembly or the Security

---

[2] Diplomatic language is based on precise wording and subtle nuances in order to avoid any misunderstandings that could cause diplomatic tensions.

Council," said a minister counselor, delegate to the Sixth Committee of the UN General Assembly.

Using simple and accessible language is essential to ensure that your message is understood unequivocally. Make sure your ideas are expressed directly, and your arguments are well structured. This will help avoid any misinterpretation of your speech.

In summary, to avoid ambiguities and misunderstandings in your statement, focus on clarity, simplicity, and precision in your language so that your message can be understood unequivocally by all the delegates present.

4.7.8. Use of Persuasion and Rhetorical Techniques

Persuasion is a powerful tool in writing your statement. Use rhetorical techniques such as using analogies, metaphors, or exaggerations to strengthen your argument.[3] Use convincing evidence, testimonies, or historical examples to support your claims. Be persuasive in your language and use strong arguments to influence your audience's opinion.

Persuasion is a valuable skill in writing your statement. To effectively convince your audience, it is recommended to use judicious rhetorical techniques. There are several ways you can strengthen your argument :

1. *Analogies and Metaphors*: Compare your topic to something familiar to your audience. For example, you could say, "Our current situation is like a boat adrift in the middle of a storm, and we need to act like the captain guiding his crew to calmer waters."

2. Exaggerations (Hyperbole): Sometimes exaggeration can be helpful in highlighting the importance of a problem. For example, "This is not just a problem for our generation, it is for future generations and is jeopardizing the future of our planet."

3. *Convincing Evidence*: Support your arguments with data, verifiable facts, and solid evidence. For example, "Statistics clearly show that this policy has led to a significant increase in the quality of life for our citizens."

4. *Testimonials*: If possible, include testimonials or personal experiences to make your speech more concrete. "Let me tell you the story of Maria, a mother who has benefited directly from our program."

---

[3] *The Use of Rhetoric in Diplomacy*: Aristotle distinguishes three types of persuasion: ethos (credibility of the speaker), logos (logic of the speech), and pathos (emotion). A good diplomatic speech combines these three elements.

5. *Historical Examples*: Support your argument by referring to similar historical events that have had significant consequences. For example, "As history has shown time and again, national unity in times of crisis can lead to extraordinary progress."
6. *Persuasive Language*: Use strong, positive language to express your ideas. Be confident and resolute in your language but remain respectful to your audience.

By using these persuasion techniques and supporting your arguments with solid evidence, you will increase the likelihood of information.

4.7.9. Impactful Conclusion

End your statement with a concise but impactful conclusion. Summarize your key points and go back to the purpose of your speech. You can conclude by calling for action or leaving a lasting reflection. For example, "In conclusion, it

Illustration of a Multilateral Meeting That Took Place Outside the Premises of the United Nations

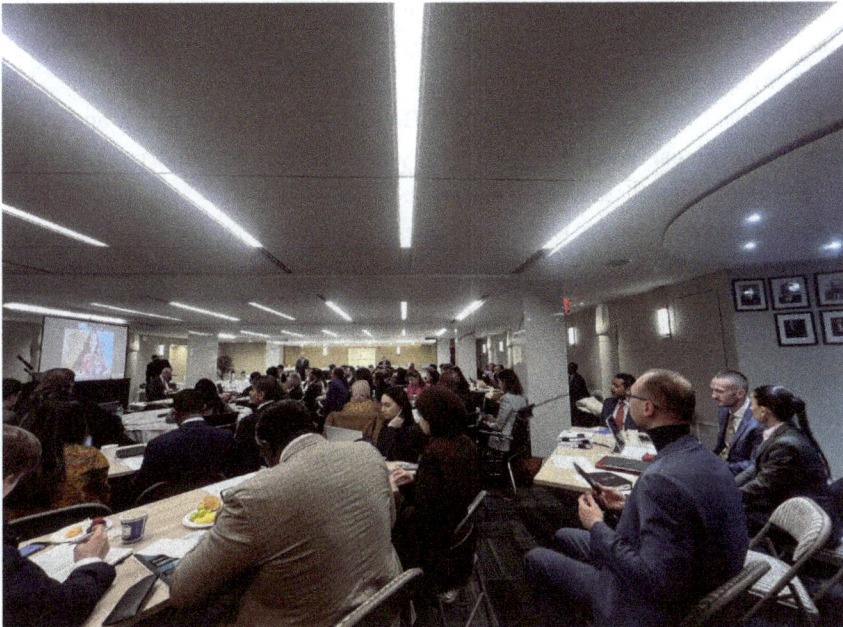

is imperative that we work together to fight climate change, because our planet depends on our actions."

By structuring your statement clearly and consistently, you will help your audience follow your speech and fully understand your points of view. This methodical approach is particularly crucial in a diplomatic context where precision and understanding are essential to reaching meaningful agreements and resolutions.

4.7.10. Review and Repetition

After writing your statement for a multilateral meeting, it is essential to dedicate time to revision and rehearsal. This step ensures that your message is clear, consistent, and impactful. Here are the steps you should take to effectively review your return:

First, *Reread Your Statement Carefully* for any inconsistencies in your arguments or misexpressed ideas. Make sure your main message is clear and that your key points are well developed.

Check Spelling, Grammar, and Punctuation: Language mistakes can distract the audience and damage the credibility of your speech. Use spell and grammar check tools if necessary.

Make Sure the Structure of Your Return Makes Sense: Your ideas should flow smoothly, with a punchy introduction, well-developed key points, and a concise yet impactful conclusion. Use logical connectors to connect your ideas in a coherent way.

Check the Clarity of Your Language: Be sure to use simple words and avoid complex technical terms. The goal is for your message to be understandable by all delegates, regardless of their expertise in the field.

Practice Your Statement Out Loud: Rehearsal allows you to familiarize yourself with the content of your speech and ensure that you can deliver it smoothly. You can also reach out to colleagues or advisors for feedback.

Be Aware of How Long You Want to Report: In multilateral meetings, speaking time is often limited. Make sure your return is within the allotted time. If necessary, adjust the length of your speech accordingly.

Ask Others for Feedback: Have your statement proofread by colleagues or advisors. Their feedback can help you identify areas for improvement or weak points that you may have missed.

By following these review and rehearsal steps, you increase your chances of delivering a compelling and impactful diplomatic statement at the multilateral meeting. Careful preparation and careful revision are essential for success in this demanding environment.

4.8. Who Prepares the Returns?

As part of the drafting of this guide, we informally approached about twenty diplomats in relation to the practice of preparing or writing interventions within their respective delegations. It was noted that the preparation of statements for speakers may vary depending on each delegation and its internal procedures. Generally, the responsibility for preparing declarations lies with the delegation itself. This can be done by members of the delegation, such as diplomats, policy experts, or advisors, who work collaboratively to draft the declaration.

In many cases, we will see that the delegations' statements are prepared in consultation with the relevant foreign ministries or agencies of each country. The representatives of the delegation discussed the topics to be discussed, the messages to be conveyed and the positions to be defended. They are based on national policies and priorities, as well as directives issued by the relevant government authorities.

The preparation of declarations may involve in-depth research, analysis of other countries' issues and positions, as well as coordination with other delegations to find commonalities or strategic alliances. Statements should be clear, concise, and consistent with national policies and the objectives of the delegation.

It is important to note that not all delegations have the same resources or capacity to prepare statements. Large delegations often have dedicated teams, experienced diplomatic services, and additional resources to assist them in the preparation of statements. Smaller or less developed delegations may have more limited resources, which may influence how their statements are prepared.

However, it is essential that all delegations can prepare their statements in a fair and balanced manner. Multilateral organizations, such as the UN, encourage the participation and representation of all delegations and strive to create an environment conducive to the expression of different voices and perspectives. It should be noted that this general description may vary depending on the specificities of each delegation and the internal rules of each multilateral organization.

The most essential habits and techniques used by diplomats in multilateral contexts are detailed in Table 3.

Table 3: Key Practices of Multilateral Diplomacy

Practice	Explanation	Benefits	Examples
Active Listening	Give the speaker full attention and ensure that all concerns are understood	Builds trust and understanding	Discussions at UN Security Council meetings
Compromise	Finding common ground that satisfies multiple parties	Resolves conflicts without escalating tensions	Peace negotiations in post-conflict regions
Flexibility	Adjust positions as needed to accommodate others	Promotes the progress of negotiations	Climate negotiations: where countries adjust their emissions targets

4.8.1. Reporting Practices Within the Institutions

As we mentioned, we conducted a survey of speakers in various multilateral meetings and among some twenty delegates from various committees of the General Assembly. These interviews allowed me to gather information on the practice of drafting declarations within their respective Mission or their respective institution to which they are attached. Based on the information collected, we manage to make the following categorization.

4.8.2. Self-writing

Several speakers, particularly those in high-level positions in their delegations, and even those in the lowest position but who were entitled to speak on behalf of his delegation, prepared and drafted their own statements. They are responsible for developing the content, structure, and tone of the statement, considering the objectives of their delegation. This drafting practice is much more common in small delegations, which are those in developing countries. This declaration is then corrected and amended by the head of mission, if necessary, before being validated. In some cases, this declaration may be sent to the capital for validation depending on the nature of its content and the issues at stake. This practice is much more prevalent in smaller, smaller missions.

4.8.3. Internal Editorial Team

The in-house editorial team within a delegation is an asset in ensuring the quality and consistency of official statements. This is indeed the case for several delegations. Composed of members who specialize in diplomatic drafting,[4] this team works closely with the designated speaker to formulate statements that accurately reflect the delegation's objectives and key messages. This approach ensures that the declaration is drafted in appropriate diplomatic language, which considers political nuances and cultural sensitivities. Additionally, the in-house drafting team can help structure the statement logically and coherently, ensuring that each point is developed in a clear and compelling manner. However, it should be noted that this practice is not widespread and only a handful of delegations have such a dedicated team. Those that do often have a competitive advantage in diplomatic communication, which enhances their ability to influence debates and advocate on the international stage.

4.8.4. Ministry of Foreign Affairs

 In many cases, delegations collaborate with their ministries of foreign affairs or other relevant government agencies. These departments provide policy advice, strategic direction, and guidance on the drafting of statements. They can also contribute to the drafting of parts of the declaration, especially when it comes to sensitive issues or key national policies. In some cases, statements completely written by the capital are sent to delegations through the Ministry of Foreign Affairs. The delegate or diplomat just must read the statement. This practice is much more common in large Permanent Missions, which nevertheless have a much more significant staff and a greater level of attention from their country to any issue.

[4.] *The Principles of Diplomatic Drafting*: A good diplomatic text follows the "rule of the three Cs":

  ✓ *Clarity*: Avoid ambiguity.
  ✓ *Conciseness*: Reduce the risk of multiple interpretations.
  ✓ *Courtesy*: Maintain a diplomatic tone, even when dissenting.

4.8.5. Consultation with Experts

Some speakers consult with internal or external experts in specific areas related to the topic of their statement. These experts bring their expertise and specialized knowledge to ensure that the statement is based on specific facts and strong arguments. In some cases, particularly during the negotiation of international legal instruments, the speeches made by diplomats may be drafted in their entirety by internal or external experts.

By following these tips when writing your statement, you will be able to convey your ideas with clarity, persuasion, and impact at multilateral meetings. In the next part of this guide, we will take a detailed look at how your statement is presented, covering aspects such as time management, managing stage fright, using visuals, and interacting with the audience.

4.9. Speaking as Chair of Sessions

As the Chairman, you play a critical role in the smooth running of multilateral meetings. Your speaking is particularly important because it guides participants, maintains order, and fosters an environment of constructive dialogue. Let us consider these few key points to consider when speaking as the Chairman.

Start with a brief introduction to welcome participants and provide context for the purpose of the session. Introduce yourself as the Chair of the session and explain the rules and procedure. Next, announce the planned agenda and the items to be discussed in the session to allow participants to prepare and understand the structure of the meeting.

Inform participants of the time allotted for each agenda item, reminding participants regularly of these deadlines to maintain the pace of the meeting. Specify the rules and procedures for speaking at the meeting, including the use of microphones, inclusion on a list of speakers, limitation of speaking time, and the need to speak in one of the official languages of the organization.

As the session Chair, make sure to maintain order and ensure mutual respect among participants. If disruptive behavior occurs, intervene calmly and assertively to restore discipline and mutual respect.

Facilitate exchanges by encouraging participants to express themselves and exchange their points of view. Give a balanced voice to the different delegations and ensure that everyone can express their ideas clearly and concisely.

Periodically, summarize the key points made in the session to ensure that all participants understand them correctly. If necessary, clarify the questions or positions expressed to avoid misunderstandings.

Conclude the session by summarizing the results achieved and providing an overview of next steps. Thank participants for their contributions and encourage them to continue working together to achieve common goals.

As a chairperson, your speech must be clear, impartial, and oriented toward the effective management of the meeting. Make sure all participants feel heard and respected, and facilitate an environment conducive to decision-making and problem-solving. Your role is crucial to ensuring the smooth running of multilateral meetings and to promote fruitful results.

4.9.1. Chairperson's Remarks

In many multilateral meetings, particularly at the UN, the remarks of the Chair of the session are prepared in collaboration with the Secretariat of the organization or institution concerned. The Secretariat plays an important role in the preparation of the speeches and interventions of the Chairperson, providing logistical support and ensuring consistency with the objectives of the meeting. In most cases, the Chairman of the meeting receives from the Secretariat everything he or she is required to say during the meeting, starting with greetings and ending with the last word on the eve of the meeting. The Secretariat typically prepares the Chair's remarks process as follows:

Coordination Meeting: There may be different ways of doing things from one international institution to another. Nevertheless, in general, the Chairperson and the Secretariat meet to discuss the agenda, the topics to be addressed and the specific objectives of the meeting. The Secretariat can also provide information on the positions of different delegations and the key points to be highlighted.

Information Gathering: The secretariat collects relevant information on the topics to be discussed at the meeting. This may involve searching for reference documents, studies, or reports prepared by experts or working groups.

Initial Drafting: Based on discussions with the president of the session or not, the secretariat drafts a first draft of the remarks to be delivered. This can include the introduction to the meeting, the points to be discussed, the specific objectives, reminders of the rules of conduct, and the thanks.

Review and Editing: The Chair reviews the first draft of the statements prepared by the Secretariat, but not in all cases. They can make changes, additions, or deletions based on their own vision, priorities, and communication style.

Finalization: Once the adjustments have been made, the secretariat finalizes the Chair's remarks by making them more formal, ensuring consistency in tone and language. The final text is then sent to the presiding officer for final approval. However, in many cases, the Chairman of the meeting only must read the document prepared by the Secretariat, which contains every word that the President has to say, starting with the greeting and the closing word.

It is important to note that the degree of involvement of the secretariat in the preparation of the Chair's remarks may vary depending on the circumstances and the importance of the meeting. In some cases, the presiding officer may write his or her own remarks based on the information provided by the secretariat.

The main objective of the preparation of the Chair's remarks by the secretariat is to ensure the clarity, precision, and consistency of the messages delivered at the meeting. This ensures effective communication between the session Chair and the participants, as well as the successful implementation of the meeting's objectives and decisions. The secretariat is expected to have a better understanding of the topics covered.

CHAPTER 5

Reporting Techniques

As we have stated on several occasions, multilateral meetings are crucial platforms where world leaders and national representatives come together to discuss and resolve issues of international importance. The effectiveness of communication at these meetings is of particular importance, as it can influence decisions, diplomatic relations, and national and international public opinion.

In this chapter, we focus on the presentation of your statement at multilateral meetings. How you deliver your message is just as important as its content. We will address key aspects such as time management, stage fright management, use of visual aids, interaction with the audience, and mastery of nonverbal communication. We also offer good communication practices that can enhance the impact of interventions at these events, covering aspects such as gestures, dress, voice rate,[1] breathing techniques, and eye contact.

5.1. Time Management

At multilateral meetings, the time allotted for each statement is usually limited. So, it is essential to manage your time effectively. Identify the key points you want to address and prioritize them. Practice your statement to make sure you stay within the allotted time and avoid unnecessary digressions. Be concise, but make sure to convey your main ideas clearly and completely. Generally, the time allotted to each speaker depends on the nature of the meeting.

An African diplomat replied:

> *To manage the time allotted, we make sure to scrupulously respect the guidelines and rules established by the chair of the meeting. We prepare our speeches according to the time allotted, making sure to prioritize our most important points*

---

[1] *The Effects of Voice and Tone in Diplomacy*: Calm and composed speech can be more effective than passionate speech. Angela Merkel is known for her moderate tone, which reinforces her authority and credibility.

Statement by a Representative of Haiti to the Third Committee During
a Meeting Where the Speaking Time Was Set at Five Minutes

and communicate them concisely. We are also flexible and ready to adjust our
discourse according to the needs and requirements of the meeting.

5.2. Management of Stage Fright

Even experienced diplomats may feel a certain nervousness before speaking
at multilateral meetings. To manage stage fright, prepare yourself properly by
practicing your declaration in advance. Take a deep breath and stay calm. Visualize yourself giving a great presentation. Remember that you are a qualified
diplomatic representative and have valuable ideas to share.

5.3. Use of Visual Aids

Using visual aids such as PowerPoint slides can enhance the impact of your
statement. Use charts, images, and diagrams to illustrate your key points and
make your presentation more dynamic. Make sure your visuals are clear, simple,
and easily readable. Do not clutter your slides with too much information and
use them only to support your speech, not to replace it.

5.4. Interaction with the Audience

Interaction with the audience is an important aspect of the presentation at multilateral meetings. Encourage interaction by asking relevant questions to the audience or inviting comments or feedback. Pay attention to the audience's reactions and adapt your speech accordingly. Show interest in others' perspectives and be open to constructive dialogue.

5.5. Mastery of Nonverbal Communication

Nonverbal communication plays a crucial role in the presentation. Use confident body language,[2] maintaining eye contact with the audience and adopting an open posture. Control your voice by speaking clearly and clearly. Use natural gestures to reinforce your words, but avoid distracting or excessive gestures. Be aware of your facial expression, which should reflect confidence and commitment.

By applying these tips when presenting your statement, you will be able to captivate your audience, convey your message effectively, and build strong connections with other diplomatic representatives. In the final part of this guide, we will discuss the importance of assessing and continuously improving your reporting skills in the multilateral context.

5.5.1. Gestures and Body Language

Positive body language is essential to strengthen communication at multilateral meetings. Workers must be aware of their gestures and posture. They should adopt a confident and open stance, avoiding appearing too rigid or too relaxed. Gestures should be used to emphasize important points in a natural way, without becoming a distraction. For example, open hand gestures can express openness and transparency, while more closed gestures can show firmness. To deepen this question, I recommend that you read the text "The Manual Gesture Associated with Language" by Cresswell (1968). In this article, he explores the relationship between manual gestures and human language by examining how hand gestures, often involuntary, can accompany and reinforce verbal communication.

[2.] *Body Language in Diplomacy*: Body language is a central part of diplomatic communication. The image of Barack Obama shaking hands with Raúl Castro in 2016 symbolized the détente between the US and Cuba after decades of tensions.

The author observes that manual gestures are an intrinsic element of human communication and can play an essential role in the transmission of information and emotions. He explains that these gestures can be used to illustrate, clarify, or reinforce oral speech. For example, a hand gesture to show the size of something during an explanation can make the message more understandable.

One participant in this study told us:

> To maximize the impact of our speeches at the United Nations, we attach great importance to delivery and presentation. We practice delivering our speech with confidence and conviction, making sure to maintain eye contact with our audience. We also use nonverbal communication techniques, such as appropriate gestures and confident posture, to reinforce our message.

Cresswell also highlights the fact that manual gestures are often culturally specific, meaning that their meaning can vary from culture to culture. He also points out that gestures are sometimes used unconsciously, which can give clues about the emotions or intentions of the person speaking. Other important texts such as those of Kristeva (1968), Lurçat (1973), and Waswo (2011) are also important to explore this question.

In summary, Robert Cresswell's text explores the role of manual gestures in human communication, highlighting their ability to accompany and enrich verbal language. Hand gestures are considered an essential part of communication and can vary in meaning depending on culture and emotional expression.

5.5.2. Appropriate Dress

Clothing is a crucial part of visual communication. Speakers should dress appropriately for the situation and level of formality of the meeting. Neat and professional attire enhances the speaker's credibility and shows respect for the participants. For example, during diplomatic meetings, traditional costumes or outfits may be required. This is a question that is addressed by many authors such as Jollet (2012), Archambault-Küch (2022), and Lequesne (2021), which shows the importance of dress in the context of diplomatic relations.

5.5.3. Throughput and Clarity

The rate of speech is a crucial element in ensuring optimal understanding at multi-lateral meetings. Stakeholders are strongly encouraged to adopt a communication approach characterized by clarity, slowness, and precise articulation. Avoiding rushing speech is particularly beneficial, as it gives participants the opportunity to easily follow the speech, thus promoting a smoother assimilation of the information presented. In addition, the judicious integration of strategic pauses is an effective technique, allowing the audience to reflect on key points, thus strengthening the impact and retention of the message conveyed (Leloir 1886).

5.5.4. Breathing Techniques

The adoption of controlled breathing techniques is of paramount importance to maintain emotional stability and vocal clarity during procedures. Before speaking, it is recommended that speakers use deep breathing techniques to promote relaxation and concentration. During the speech, regular and deep breathing is essential to maintain a stable and confident voice, thus enhancing the impact and confidence of communication. This practice also helps to control any signs of nervousness, thus offering the workers greater control over their oral expression.[3]

5.5.5. Eye Contact

Eye contact is a powerful way to connect with the audience. Interveners should try to maintain eye contact with different members of the hearing. This shows

---

[3] Here are some notable authors in the field of diplomatic communication and international relations that you may want to consider consulting that could broaden your scope of expertise in this area.

1. *Edward Hall*: American anthropologist whose work on cross-cultural communication can provide important insights.
2. *Erving Goffman*: Canadian sociologist, best known for his contributions to the theory of social interaction, could offer insights on self-presentation in a diplomatic context.
3. *Joseph Nye*: American political scientist who developed the concept of "soft power" that can be relevant to modern diplomacy.
4. *Herbert Kelman*: American psychologist specializing in conflict resolution and negotiation.
5. *Edward Luttwak*: Strategist and historian of international relations, his work can be useful in addressing geopolitical issues.
6. *Madeleine Albright*: A former U.S. Secretary of State, her memoirs and writings on diplomacy could provide practical perspectives.
7. *Richard N. Haass*: President of the Council on Foreign Relations, his work covers various aspects of international relations.
8. *George Lakoff*: American cognitive linguist, his research on rhetoric and language could be relevant to persuasive communication.
9. *Shashi Tharoor*: Indian diplomat and author, his thoughts on diplomacy and international relations can offer a non-Western perspective.
10. *Michel Foucault*: French philosopher, his ideas on power and governance can be applied to the analysis of international dynamics.

commitment and care toward the participants. For example, at the 70th session of the UN General Assembly in 2015, U.S. President Barack Obama's speech was praised for his confident body language and eye contact with the audience, reinforcing his speech's impact on the Sustainable Development Goals. Also, Nelson Mandela, during his historic speeches, was known for his slow flow and mastery of eye contact, creating a powerful connection with his audience and reinforcing his messages of reconciliation and unity in South Africa.

5.5.6. Managing Emotions

Managing emotions is an important aspect of communication at multilateral meetings. Stakeholders may be confronted with tense situations or disagreements, and maintaining self-control and diplomacy is essential. Avoid negative facial expressions or inflammatory comments. Instead, remain calm, respectful, and open to dialogue.

Table 4 is an example of a table describing different presentation techniques for delivering statements at diplomatic meetings.

Table 4: Presentation Techniques for Diplomatic Interventions

Technique	Tools Used	Benefits	Examples
Use of visual aids	PowerPoint, Precise	Improves compre-hension, maintains attention	Graphics, images in a slideshow
Structured delivery	Notes, Teleprompter	Ensures clarity, keeps speech on track	Numbered or bulleted list of key points
Engagement de l'audience	Polls, Q&A Sessions	Increases partici-pation, makes the session interactive	Live polls, directed questions
Narration	Anecdotes, Examples	Makes content re-latable, Improves retention	Personal stories, case studies

This table offers a summary of presentation techniques with descriptions and examples to facilitate their understanding and application. You can adjust or enrich these few techniques according to your specificities or requirements.

These communication techniques are not only crucial skills for world leaders, but they can also be applied by any individual looking to improve their communication during important meetings. The effectiveness of these practices helps to strengthen international diplomacy, foster mutual understanding, and achieve common goals in multilateral meetings.

5.6. Continuous Evaluation and Improvement

Multilateral diplomacy requires constant reflection and continuous improvement of diplomatic skills. Diplomatic representatives, when speaking at multilateral meetings, must assess their performance to identify strengths to maintain and weaknesses to improve. In the fifth and final part of your guide, we focus on assessing your reporting skills in the multilateral context and ways to continuously improve your performance. This step is crucial to strengthen your effectiveness and influence at multilateral meetings. We will cover aspects such as self-assessment, seeking feedback, continuous training, and adapting to changes in the diplomatic landscape.

5.6.1. Strengths and Weaknesses to Be Considered

Diplomatic excellence in multilateral meetings is based on continuous self-assessment and continuous improvement of skills. Here, we explore the strengths and weaknesses that diplomats and stakeholders in multilateral meetings need to identify and address to maximize their impact in diplomatic forums. By highlighting these elements, we offer insight into the crucial aspects that shape diplomatic success, illustrated by concrete examples of how these elements can influence outcomes in the multilateral context. This is intended to encourage constructive thinking and support the continuous improvement of diplomatic skills. Without going into detail, we provide here a non-exhaustive list of strengths and weaknesses to identify and act accordingly.

5.6.1.1. Strengths to Be Identified and Enhanced

When leaders, diplomats, and other stakeholders speak at multilateral meetings, it is essential to recognize and value their strengths. These strengths are the assets, skills and characteristics that contribute to enhancing their credibility, positively influencing national and international public opinion, and promoting the success of negotiations and discussions. Identifying and highlighting these strengths is an effective strategy to maximize the impact of speeches and interventions at these international forums.

In this section, we will explore the different strengths that speakers may possess and how to best identify and value them. Whether it is the relevance of experience, the ability to communicate effectively, the mastery of complex subjects, or other specific skills, these assets can play a crucial role in creating an environment conducive to diplomacy and international cooperation.

5.6.1.2. Mastery of Files or Technical Expertise

Diplomats who have a thorough knowledge of the topics under discussion are able to argue in a solid way. For example, a delegate who is an expert in international trade can positively influence trade negotiations. If the speaker has technical expertise in a specific area related to the meeting agenda, they can use this as a highlight. The audience often places a high value on in-depth knowledge of a topic.

5.6.1.3. Diplomatic Language

The use of appropriate diplomatic language is essential to maintaining good relations. For example, instead of accusing directly, a diplomat can express concerns using terms such as "we wish to emphasize" or "we would like to discuss." Diplomatic language, also known as language diplomacy, is a crucial aspect of international diplomacy.[4] It refers to the use of specific, formal, and respectful language in communications and negotiations between representatives of different countries. Here are some key characteristics of diplomatic language:

1. *Formality*: Diplomatic language is generally very formal. Diplomats use honorific titles, courtesies, and expressions of courtesy to show respect for their interlocutors.

---

[4] Until the nineteenth century, Latin was the main language of international treaties. From the Treaty of Rastatt (1714), French became the main diplomatic language, before being gradually replaced by English after the World War II.

2. *Neutrality*: Diplomats avoid taking a partisan position. They use neutral and objective language to discuss international issues and conflicts.[5]

3. *Accuracy*: Accuracy is key in diplomacy. Terms and agreements must be clearly defined to avoid ambiguity. Diplomats often use specific legal formulations.

4. *Reservation*: Diplomats are often cautious in their words and writings. They avoid impulsive or provocative statements that could inflame diplomatic tensions.

5. *Confidentiality*: Diplomatic discussions are often confidential. Diplomats are tight-lipped about the details of the ongoing negotiations and their government's positions.

6. *Official Languages*: In the context of international organizations such as the UN, there are specific official languages for diplomatic communications. This ensures that all parties understand the official documents and statements.

7. *Protocol*: Diplomatic protocol includes specific rules and customs regarding the order of speeches, greetings, titles, and other aspects of diplomatic behavior.

8. *Cooperation*: Although diplomatic language may seem rigid, it is intended to facilitate international cooperation. It allows diplomats to discuss sensitive issues in a civilized and constructive manner.

Diplomatic language is essential for establishing international relations, negotiating treaties, resolving conflicts, and facilitating understanding between nations. It reflects the values of diplomacy, including preventive diplomacy, coercive diplomacy, and mediation diplomacy.[6] Diplomats trained in the use of this language are well equipped to represent their country effectively on the international stage.

5.6.1.4. Ability to Build Alliances

Multilateral diplomacy often relies on the creation of coalitions and alliances. A diplomat who can bring together countries that share common interests can

---

[5] *The Importance of Neutrality in Diplomatic Writing*: In diplomacy, neutral language helps to limit tensions. For example, the UN Charter uses terms such as "recognize" rather than "condemn" to avoid diplomatic deadlocks.

[6] *The Use of Diplomatic Mediation*: Kofi Annan, former UN Secretary-General, led mediation missions to Syria and Côte d'Ivoire, demonstrating the importance of quiet diplomacy.

influence decisions. For example, in regional security negotiations, a delegate may create an alliance between neighboring countries to promote stability.

Indeed, the ability to create alliances is a crucial skill in the field of diplomacy and international relations. It involves the ability to build successful partnerships and collaborations between different nations, organizations, or groups of actors in order to advance common interests, solve global problems, or address complex challenges. We offer a few key elements related to this skill:

1. *Diplomacy*: Diplomacy is the art of negotiating and engaging constructively with other countries. Diplomats and government officials must be able to build positive relationships with their foreign counterparts and find areas of agreement.

2. *Leadership*: Building alliances requires effective leadership. Leaders need to inspire trust, lead the way, and motivate stakeholders to work together.

3. *Communication*: Effective communication is key to explaining the benefits of collaboration and resolving misunderstandings. This includes intercultural communication, proficiency in foreign languages, and the ability to express oneself clearly.

4. *Negotiation Skills*: Skilled negotiators can find mutually beneficial compromises and resolve disagreements constructively.

5. *Knowledge of International Issues*: Understanding global issues, such as international trade, security, the environment, and human rights, is essential to identify areas where cooperation is needed.

6. *Networking*: Establishing a large network of contacts is valuable for building alliances. Diplomats and international actors interact regularly with people from diverse backgrounds.

7. *Conflict Management*: Disputes and disagreements can arise within alliances. Knowing how to manage conflicts constructively is essential to maintaining solidarity.

8. *Flexibility and Adaptability*: International situations change rapidly. The ability to adapt to changing circumstances is important for maintaining alliances.

9. *Mediation Skills*: In the event of disagreement within an alliance, the ability to mediate can be valuable in preserving cohesion.

10. *Commitment to the Common Goal*: The willingness to work toward a common goal is the foundation of successful alliances. Participants must put aside their individual interests in favor of the collective goal.

Examples of effective alliance-building in history include the formation of the UN to promote world peace after World War II, international climate change agreements such as the Paris Agreement, and military and humanitarian coalitions to respond to global crises. The ability to build alliances is a major asset in today's complex and interconnected world, where transnational problems often require cooperative solutions.

5.6.1.5. Conflict Management

Diplomacy inevitably involves disagreements. Diplomats who can manage these conflicts constructively and seek balanced solutions are valuable. For example, in negotiations on shared water resources, a delegate may facilitate a fair agreement. Therefore, conflict management is an essential skill in the field of diplomacy and international relations. It involves the ability to prevent, resolve, and mitigate conflicts between different parties, whether at the national or international level. Below are some key elements related to this skill:

1. *Conflict Analysis*: The first step in conflict management is to understand the causes and underlying dynamics of conflict. It is essential to analyze in depth the political, economic, social, and cultural factors that contribute to tensions (Postel-Vinay et al. 2013).
2. *Effective Communication*: Communication plays a crucial role in conflict prevention and resolution. Mediators must be able to facilitate dialogue between the parties to the conflict, ensure that each other's concerns are heard, and promote mutual understanding.
3. *Negotiation*: Negotiation skills are essential for reaching agreements and compromises that satisfy all parties involved. This involves finding win-win solutions and resolving disagreements peacefully. "Negotiation and the rule as the product of an agreement after negotiation are generally seen as the two central concepts of the approach Reynaldian of conflict and regulation. For its part, the strategic analysis of organizations is commonly identified with the conceptual couple of power and strategy" (Friedberg 2009, 15).
4. *Mediation*: In many conflicts, third-party mediators are needed to facilitate talks and help the parties reach an agreement. Mediation requires neutrality, impartiality and a thorough understanding of the conflict.

5. *Crisis Management*: In crisis situations, effective management is crucial to avoid an escalation of the conflict. This may include actions to de-escalate tensions, protect civilians, and facilitate peace talks (Lagadec 2012).[7]

6. *Preventive Diplomacy*: The goal of preventive diplomacy is to identify and address potential sources of conflict before they reach a critical stage. This requires constant monitoring of tense situations and putting measures in place to proactively resolve them.

7. *Knowledge of International Agreements and Norms:* A thorough understanding of international law, treaties and norms is important to guide conflict resolution toward solutions that are consistent with international law.

8. 8. *Managing Cultural Diversity*: In international conflicts, cultural differences can be a source of tension. Cultural sensitivity and the ability to work with people from diverse backgrounds are essential.

9. *Emergency Management*: When conflict erupts suddenly, a rapid and coordinated response is needed to protect civilian populations and find short-term solutions.

10. *Ethics*: Conflict management must be guided by ethical principles, such as respect for human rights and the protection of vulnerable populations.

Examples of successful conflict management in the international context include peace agreements such as the Dayton Accords that ended the war in Bosnia, as well as UN peacekeeping missions in conflict zones such as Darfur.

Conflict management is a crucial skill in promoting peace, stability, and international cooperation. It requires a combination of analytical, communication, and mediation skills, as well as a thorough understanding of political and cultural issues.

5.6.1.6. Persuasive Communication

The ability to persuade other delegates to support a proposal or idea is an asset. For example, in discussions on reducing greenhouse gas emissions, a delegate may present compelling data on environmental and economic benefits. This makes persuasive communication an essential skill in the field of diplomacy and international relations. It involves positively influencing the opinion, decisions,

---

[7] A good example of crisis diplomacy is that of Secretary of State Henry Kissinger during the Yom Kippur War (1973), who used "shuttle diplomacy" to de-escalate the conflict between Israel and Arab countries.

and actions of other parties, whether individuals, groups, or governments, using strong arguments, effective persuasion techniques, and persuasive communication. Here are some key elements related to this skill:

1. *Establish Credibility*: To be persuasive, a communicator must establish their own credibility. This involves showing that you are knowledgeable, honest, and trustworthy. Background, skills, and expertise are important elements in building credibility.

2. *Know Your Audience*: To be persuasive, it is essential to understand the needs, values, and concerns of your target audience. This allows you to tailor your message in a way that makes it more relevant to them.

3. *Use Strong Arguments*: Persuasion is based on strong arguments and convincing evidence. It is important to present facts, data, and concrete examples to support your point of view.

4. *Use Rhetoric Effectively*: Rhetoric is the art of convincing and per-suading through speech. It includes techniques such as using analogies, metaphors, historical allusions, and emotional speeches to reinforce your message.

5. *Arouse Emotions*: Emotions have a powerful impact on persuasion. Using emotional narratives, personal testimonials, and real-life examples can spark empathy and emotional engagement in your audience.

6. *Avoid Confrontation*: Persuasive communication is about convincing, not provoking conflict. It is important to avoid offensive or condescending language that could alienate your audience.

7. *Use Diplomacy*: In the context of diplomacy, persuasive communication plays a critical role in influencing international negotiations, agreements, and political decisions. Diplomats must be able to defend their country's interests convincingly while maintaining constructive relations with other parties.

8. *Know When to Listen*: Persuasion is not just about talking, it is about listening. Understanding other parties' concerns and perspectives can strengthen your ability to persuade them.

9. *Adapt to Communication Channels*: Persuasive communication can be done through a variety of channels, including speeches, articles, in-person meetings, social media, and formal negotiations. It is important to choose the appropriate channels based on the audience and the purpose.

10. *Measure Effectiveness*: To assess the effectiveness of your persuasive communication, it is important to monitor reactions and results. This can include gathering feedback, observing changes in attitude and behavior, and adapting your approach accordingly.

Persuasive communication is used in many diplomatic contexts, including influencing policy decisions, mobilizing international support, promoting peace agreements, and defending national interests. Diplomats and international leaders who excel in this skill are often able to shape public opinion, influence policy, and contribute to solving global problems.

5.6.1.7. Networks and Relationships

Networks and relationships play an essential role in diplomacy and international relations. Diplomats, national leaders, and international actors need to establish and maintain strong networks to achieve their goals, whether it is to promote peace, negotiate agreements, cooperate on global issues, or defend national interests. We give some key aspects related to this skill:

1. *Establishment of Diplomatic Relations*: Diplomats are responsible for establishing and maintaining diplomatic relations with other countries. This includes the creation of formal channels of communication, such as embassies and consulates, as well as the development of personal relationships with foreign diplomats.
2. *Personal Networks*: Diplomats and international leaders often develop personal networks of contacts around the world. These contacts may include diplomatic colleagues, foreign government officials, international relations experts, representatives of international organizations, members of civil society, and other relevant actors.
3. *Public Diplomacy*: Public relations and communication with the general public are increasingly important in modern diplomacy.[8] Diplomats often use traditional and social media to promote their countries, share information, and influence international public opinion.

---

[8] *A diplomatic spokesperson is responsible for communicating the official position of a state, while managing the expectations of the public and the media.*

4. *Economic Diplomacy*: Economic and trade relations are crucial for many countries. Diplomats work to promote foreign investment, negotiate trade agreements, foster international trade, and strengthen economic partnerships.

5. *Multilateral Diplomacy*: Multilateral diplomacy involves creating and maintaining relationships with international organizations such as the UN, the European Union, NATO, the World Trade Organization (WTO), and others. These relationships are essential for influencing global policies and cooperating on international issues.

6. *Alliance Management*: Countries are forming strategic alliances to strengthen their security and position on the international stage. Diplomats are responsible for managing these alliances, coordinating policies with allies, and working together on common issues.

7. *Conflict Resolution*: Networks and relationships are often used to facilitate conflict resolution. Mediators, facilitators, and negotiators use their connections to bring conflicting parties to the negotiating table.

8. *Cultural Diplomacy*: Cultural diplomacy aims to promote intercultural understanding and cultural exchanges between countries. Diplomats promote cultural events, exhibitions, educational programs and cultural partnerships.

9. *Global Health Diplomacy*: Networks and relationships are critical in global health diplomacy, as we have seen during the COVID-19 pandemic. Countries are working with the World Health Organization (WHO) and other partners to address global health crises.

10. *Coalition-Building*: In the field of international security, countries often seek to form coalitions to address common threats. The ability to build and maintain effective coalitions is a key competency.

In short, networks and relationships are at the heart of diplomacy and international relations. They enable international actors to influence policies, build partnerships, resolve conflicts, and cooperate on global issues. The ability to build and manage these relationships is essential for success in diplomacy.

5.6.2. Weaknesses to Be Identified and Improved

In this complex and demanding field, awareness of one's vulnerabilities and the willingness to improve are essential for success. Here, we will explore some of the common pain points that diplomats and international relations actors may encounter, as well as tips for overcoming them.

Diplomacy is a dynamic field where the stakes are high and competition for influence and international cooperation is constant. Diplomatic actors must not only understand the complexities of international relations but also master a range of interpersonal and strategic skills to succeed. However, no one is without its weaknesses, and diplomats, whether novice or seasoned, can benefit from identifying and improving their shortcomings.

In the following sections, we will look in detail at various potential pain points, from lack of language skills to difficulty managing conflict to persuasive communication. We will also offer practical advice and strategies to develop these skills and strengthen your impact in the field of diplomacy and international relations.

Whether you are an aspiring diplomat or a seasoned veteran, this section will provide you with useful information to identify and overcome your weaknesses, strengthen your skills, and succeed in this crucial area where actions and decisions have a global impact. Here we give some common weak points to watch out for and work on to succeed in diplomacy:

1. *Insufficient Language Skills*: Diplomacy often requires proficiency in several foreign languages. If a diplomat has limited language skills, this can be a barrier to effective communication and negotiation.

2. *Lack of International Experience*: International experience is valuable in diplomacy. Individuals who have not had the opportunity to live or work abroad may lack international prospects.

3. *Lack of Negotiation Skills*: Diplomacy relies heavily on the ability to negotiate. A weak point in this area can make it difficult to reach agreements and resolve conflicts.

4. *Inadequate Communication*: Diplomatic communication requires a high degree of precision and an understanding of cultural nuances. Inadequate communication skills can lead to misunderstandings or diplomatic incidents.

5. *Lack of Understanding of Foreign Cultures*: Diplomacy often involves interactions with foreign cultures. A lack of understanding of cultural customs, values, and norms can lead to diplomatic missteps. For example, a gesture that is considered polite in one culture may be perceived as offensive in another.

6. *Lack of Patience and Resilience*: Diplomatic negotiations can be long and difficult. A lack of patience and resilience can impair the ability to persevere in complex situations.

7. *Poor Emotional Management*: Diplomats are often confronted with tense situations. Poor emotional management can lead to inappropriate reactions or escalating conflicts.

8. *Lack of Flexibility*: Diplomacy often requires adapting quickly to changing circumstances. A lack of flexibility can hinder the ability to respond effectively.

9. *Inability to Build Alliances*: Diplomatic alliances are crucial for many countries. The inability to build strong relationships with other nations can limit diplomatic influence.

10. *Lack of Knowledge of International Issues*: Diplomats need to be well-informed about international issues. A lack of knowledge of the issues can diminish credibility.

11. *Lack of Leadership*: Diplomats often hold leadership positions. A lack of leadership skills can hinder the ability to lead teams and make important decisions.

12. *Difficulty Working in a Team*: Diplomacy often involves working with colleagues at home and abroad. Collaboration issues can affect the success of diplomatic missions.

13. *Lack of Conflict Resolution*: Diplomacy requires the resolution of conflicts, whether internal or external. The inability to manage conflicts can lead to diplomatic stalemates.

14. *Lack of Long-Term Vision*: Diplomacy requires long-term vision and strategic planning. A lack of vision can limit the ability to achieve long-term goals.

15. *Lack of Preparation*: **It is important for a worker to take the time necessary to prepare his or her intervention.** Poorly prepared statements can be incoherent and unconvincing. For example, a delegate who has not sufficiently studied the working documents may be caught off guard.

It is important to note that no one is perfect, and everyone has weaknesses at some point in their career. Identifying these weak points is the first step to improving them. Training, mentorship, experience, and constructive feedback are ways to build these skills and succeed in diplomacy.

By identifying these strengths and weaknesses, diplomats can put in place continuous improvement strategies to optimize their effectiveness in multilateral meetings. The examples given illustrate how these aspects can have an impact on diplomacy and on the outcome of negotiations.

5.6.2.1. Self-assessment

An honest and regular self-assessment of your reporting skills is essential to identify your strengths and areas for improvement. Reflect on your past performance, analyze your previous statements, and identify what worked well and what can be improved. Ask yourself key questions, such as: *Was my statement clear and consistent? Have I managed to persuade my audience? Have I used presentation techniques effectively?* This self-assessment will help guide your improvement efforts.

5.6.2.2. Seeking Feedback

Seeking feedback from colleagues, mentors, or people with experience in the diplomatic field is a valuable way to gain outside perspectives. Solicit constructive feedback on your presentation style, language, use of visuals, and overall impact. Take suggestions and criticism into account to hone your skills and continuously improve.

5.6.2.3. Formation Continue

Continuous training is essential to stay up to date with best practices and developments in the diplomatic field. Look for training opportunities, workshops, or courses that help you strengthen your reporting skills. Learn from experts, share experiences with your peers, and develop new techniques to improve your performance. Stay open to learning throughout your diplomatic journey.

5.6.2.4. Adapting to Changes in the Diplomatic Landscape

The diplomatic landscape is constantly evolving, with new issues, changing issues, and fluctuating political dynamics. It is crucial to stay informed of global developments and adapt to changes in the diplomatic context. Be prepared to adjust your approach, language, and arguments to new realities, while staying true to your core principles and values.

By putting into practice the regular evaluation of your skills, seeking feedback, engaging in continuous training, and adapting to changes in the diplomatic landscape, you will be able to continuously improve your performance in terms of declarations at multilateral meetings. Remember that *The Diplomatic Voice* is a journey of constant learning and growth, and each experience allows you to further assert yourself as a competent and influential diplomatic representative.

5.6.2.5. Conclusion and Additional Resources

From all the above, we can deduce that the drafting and presentation of statements in multinational meetings are essential skills for any diplomatic representative. By mastering these skills, you can influence decisions, promote your ideas, and actively contribute to international discussions and negotiations. This guide has covered the key aspects of writing, presenting, and continuously improving your statements, providing you with practical tips, concrete examples and effective strategies. By applying these principles, you will be able to strengthen your impact at multilateral meetings and contribute significantly to global diplomatic efforts.

To deepen your knowledge and skills in diplomacy and multilateral communication, we recommend that you consult the following complementary resources: Books on diplomacy and negotiation: Books such as *Diplomacy* by Henry Kissinger; *Getting to Yes: Negotiating an Agreement Without Giving In* by Roger Fisher and William Ury; and *The Art of Diplomacy: Strengthening the Canada-U.S. Relationship in Times of Uncertainty* by Bruce Heyman and Vicki Heyman offer valuable insights into diplomatic practice and effective communication.

Many online courses and training are available to develop your skills in diplomacy and multilateral communication. Platforms such as Coursera, edX, and Udemy offer courses on diplomacy, cross-cultural communication, negotiation, and other related topics. Look for experienced diplomatic mentors, colleagues, or professional networks who can offer additional advice, guidance, and learning opportunities. Discussions with people who have practical experience in diplomacy can be extremely enriching and help you hone your skills.

By using these complementary resources and continuing your professional development, you will continue to build your expertise in statements and make progress on *The Diplomatic Voice*.

In conclusion, this guide *The Diplomatic Voice: Mastering the Art of Multilateral Communication* has provided you with an in-depth understanding of the drafting and presentation of statements in multinational meetings. By combining this knowledge with regular practice, openness to continuous learning, and the use of complementary resources, you will be able to become an accomplished and influential diplomatic communicator. Good luck in your future multilateral meetings and in your efforts to promote international cooperation and understanding.

5.7. Some Good Practices for Multilateral Meetings

The seventh part of your guide addresses good practices to adopt at multilateral meetings. These tips will help you maximize the effectiveness of your statements and foster constructive exchanges with other diplomatic representatives.

5.7.1. Careful Preparation

Preparation is the key to success at multilateral meetings. Inform yourself about the topics on the agenda, study the positions of other countries and prepare your arguments accordingly. Identify the strengths and weaknesses of your position and plan responses to potential arguments from other delegates. The more prepared you are, the more confident and convincing you will be when making your statement.

5.7.2. Active Listening

At multilateral meetings, it is crucial to practice active listening. Pay close attention to the interventions of other representatives and be open to different points of view. Take notes to remember key ideas and use them to formulate relevant answers in subsequent discussions. Active listening promotes mutual understanding and strengthens diplomatic relations.

5.7.3. Respect and Courtesy

In multilateral meetings, it is essential to show respect and courtesy to other delegates. Avoid personal attacks or harsh criticism. Stay focused on ideas and arguments and express yourself in a respectful way even if you disagree. Mutual respect is the basis of diplomacy and facilitates the search for common solutions.

5.7.4. Coalition-Building

To enhance the impact of your statement, seek to build coalitions with other countries that share similar interests. Identify delegates who might support your position and engage in behind-the-scenes discussions to explore opportunities for cooperation. Coalitions boost the credibility of your statement and increase your chances of advancing your diplomatic goals.

5.7.5. Flexibility and Trade-Off

Multilateral diplomacy often requires compromise and flexibility. Be prepared to listen to other delegates' proposals and explore compromise solutions that could benefit all parties. Constructive dialogue and the search for common solutions are key elements for progress in multilateral negotiations.

5.7.6. Monitoring and Implementation

Once the multilateral meeting is over, be sure to follow up appropriately. Take note of the commitments made by other delegates and ensure that they are implemented. Maintain regular contact with your counterparts to monitor progress and maintain diplomatic momentum. Active monitoring helps to strengthen relationships and foster ongoing cooperation.

By integrating these good practices into your approach to multilateral meetings, you will be able to maximize the impact of your statements, foster constructive discussions, and contribute meaningfully to shared diplomatic objectives.

In conclusion, success in multilateral meetings is based on careful preparation, active listening, mutual respect, coalition-building, flexibility, monitoring, and implementation of commitments. By putting these good practices into practice, you will be able to carry out your role as a diplomatic representative competently and effectively.

5.8. Speaking Sitting or Standing

Speaking in multilateral forums is a crucial dimension of modern diplomacy, where every word spoken can have profound implications on the international stage. Speeches, whether delivered from a country's headquarters or standing in the main gallery, are powerful instruments shaping opinion, influencing debates and building crucial alliances.

In this complex world of multilateral meetings, each posture adopted by a speaker has a particular meaning. Seated speech provides a more informal setting for interactive debate, in-depth discussions, and informal exchanges. In contrast, standing at the main podium is formal and solemn, often marking decisive moments such as the presentation of national positions, the launch of major initiatives or the response to crucial issues.

Let us explore the subtleties and strategies inherent in these two modes of speaking, which are much more than formal gestures. Every choice, whether sitting to foster interaction or standing up to assert a position with authority, helps shape the dynamic landscape of international relations.

Illustration of a Seated Speech at the Fourth Committee
of the UN General Assembly

The use of a standing statement sends a strong message and helps to establish a solemn presence, emphasizing the authority and seriousness of the topics discussed. It can also captivate the audience's attention and enhance the impact of the words spoken.

5.8.1. Circumstances of Sitting or Standing

The choice between sitting or standing at multilateral meetings is often determined by established protocols. However, there are exceptional circumstances that may influence this decision. Generally, stakeholders adhere to established protocol standards to maintain formality and respect for diplomatic traditions.

Sitting is often preferred in more informal settings such as committee meetings, small group discussions, or relaxed negotiation sessions. It promotes a more relaxed exchange and can create an environment conducive to informal and open dialogues.

On the other hand, standing speech is often reserved for solemn moments, such as opening speeches, general policy statements, or formal interventions before a general assembly. This posture gives a more official character to the speech, reinforcing the weight of the words expressed.

In exceptional situations, such as unforeseen events or crises, stakeholders may sometimes be called upon to speak unexpectedly, without prior planning. These situations can influence the posture adopted depending on the urgency or informality of the speech.

In short, although the choice between sitting or standing is often determined by protocol rules, special circumstances or unforeseen situations can also play a role in the decision of the posture to adopt. Without going into detail, we provide here some circumstances that favor speaking in a standing position rather than sitting.

5.8.1.1. Major Policy Statement

A major policy statement is a way for a representative to mark the importance and seriousness of a particular topic. When a head of State or a senior official speaks standing up, it sends a clear signal about the importance and urgency of the issue being discussed. This approach is often used to announce important decisions, major reforms, or firm positions on critical issues such as international security, human rights, or diplomatic relations. By standing, the representative demonstrates his or her personal commitment and that of his or her country to the subject in question, thereby enhancing the impact and credibility of his or her words.

5.8.1.2. Official Announcements or Press Releases

Official announcements or press releases are crucial moments at multilateral meetings, as they often represent important decisions taken by the participating countries. When a representative wishes to publicly announce a treaty, agreement, or major policy measure, they may choose to do so standing up to add solemnity and authority to the announcement. This symbolic posture reinforces the seriousness of the announcement and testifies to the serious commitment of the representative and his country to the issue. By standing, the representative also communicates to other participants and the media the strength and determination of their position, which can help shape the perceptions and reactions of other actors involved.

5.8.1.3. Taking a Strong Stance

Taking a strong stand is often necessary in multilateral meetings, especially during intense debates or when a country wishes to express its firmness on a specific issue. In such situations, a representative may choose to make a standing statement to reinforce the strength and conviction of his or her speech. By standing, the representative symbolizes his or her country's commitment and determination to stand up for his or her beliefs, which can influence other participants and encourage them to take this position into account. This posture also underlines the importance of the topic at hand and can elicit a stronger reaction from other delegations, thus helping to move the debate forward and find solutions.

5.8.1.4. Moments of Commemoration or Contemplation

During moments of commemoration, mourning ceremonies, or meditation, it is common to make standing statements to mark the respect and solemnity of the occasion. This can include tributes to those who have died, moments of silence, or statements of solidarity.

Speech by the Permanent Representative of
Haiti to the United Nations at the Ceremony of Tribute
to the Late President of Haiti HE Mr. Jovenel Moise

It should be noted that circumstances may vary depending on the specific context and customs of each organization or country. Decisions regarding standing statements are usually made based on the nature of the event, the protocol, and the representative's desired impact.

5.8.1.5. Authority and Solemnity

Speeches delivered with authority and solemnity are of paramount importance at multilateral meetings. They are of a particularly serious and formal nature. It seems important to us to show how such a discourse is generally structured:

1. *Solemn Introduction*: The speech begins with a solemn introduction that immediately captures the audience's attention. The speaker may use expressions such as "Ladies and Gentlemen," "Honourable delegates," or other respectful expressions to greet the assembly.
2. *Topic Enunciation*: The speaker clearly states the topic or theme of the speech, placing it in an overall context. This step allows the audience to understand what it will be about.

3. *Presentation of the Issues*: The speech continues by exposing the issues and the implications of the subject being discussed. The speaker could emphasize the importance of the topic for the international community or the challenges it posed.
4. *Principles and Values*: The speaker can recall the fundamental principles and values that guide the country he or she represents. This shows that the country's position is in line with universal values such as human rights, justice, or peace.
5. *Country Position*: The statement then sets out the country-specific position on the issue under consideration. This position is usually expressed with firmness and conviction, thus reinforcing the solemn character of the speech.
6. *Call to Action*: The speaker can conclude the speech with a call to action. This can take the form of an invitation to cooperation, to the peaceful resolution of conflicts or to adhere to common principles.
7. *Solemn Conclusion*: The speech ends with a solemn conclusion, in which the speaker reiterates the importance of the topic and expresses gratitude to the audience for their attention.
8. *Quotes or References*: To reinforce the authority of the speech, the speaker may include quotes from renowned leaders or personalities, references to international documents or resolutions, or relevant historical examples.
9. *Formal Language*: The entire speech is formulated in formal and respectful language. The speaker avoids familiarity or informal expressions.

In short, a speech delivered with authority and solemnity is intended to make an impression at multilateral meetings. It highlights the country's position in a formal and respectful manner, while recalling its fundamental principles and values. This type of speech aims to influence and persuade the audience in a convincing way.

5.8.2. Sitting Intervention from the Country Headquarters

When speaking in a multilateral forum such as the UN General Assembly, representatives of Member States usually have the choice between sitting or standing. The decision to choose one or the other position depends on several factors, such as the nature of the speech, the personal style of the representative, and common practices observed in meetings.

Speaking from the country's headquarters in a multilateral room is a crucial moment at international meetings. It is an opportunity for a representative of a country to make their nation's voice heard, express their positions, defend their interests, and contribute to discussions and negotiations that can have a significant impact on the world stage. This usually takes place when the topic on the agenda is of direct concern to the country in question or when it wishes to share important information on international issues.

The process of intervention from the country's headquarters in a multilateral room is governed by a set of procedural rules and protocols specific to each international organization. These rules are intended to ensure a fair and orderly debate, to respect the time allotted for each intervention, and to ensure that all parties can express themselves in a fair manner.

When a representative of a country speaks from the headquarters of his delegation, he or she often has to follow a number of steps. First, he must ask to speak according to established procedures, such as raising his hand, using a microphone, or any other mechanism in place. Once recognized by the Chair of the meeting, the representative can then begin his intervention.

The procedure itself must be carefully prepared. The representative should clearly define the objectives of his speech, determining what he wants to accomplish: to influence the opinions of other delegates, to promote a specific proposal, to share crucial information, or to defend the interests of his country. Preparation also involves gathering relevant information and data on the topic at hand, conducting thorough research, and structuring the speech in a logical and coherent way.

When speaking, it is essential to adapt your speech to the audience in the multilateral room. This means understanding the interests, concerns and expectations of other delegates, and using clear and accessible language to make the message understandable to all.

Finally, intervention from the country's headquarters is often time-limited. Representatives must, therefore, be aware of this constraint and ensure that they respect the time allotted to them.

Overall, speaking from the country's headquarters in a multilateral hall is a valuable opportunity to actively participate in international debates and contribute to decision-making on global issues. It is a diplomatic act that requires careful preparation, an understanding of procedural rules, and an ability to communicate effectively to advance one's country's interests and contribute to comprehensive solutions. Certain circumstances or personal preferences may

During a Seated Intervention by the Representative
of Haiti from the Country's Headquarters

lead a representative to choose to make a seated intervention at multilateral meetings. In the following lines, we offer a few examples to illustrate when a sitting procedure may be preferred.

5.8.2.1. Informal Environment

In informal meetings or less formal discussions, it is common for participants to choose to speak seated. This posture creates a more relaxed atmosphere and encourages informal exchanges between representatives. By gathering around a table or in a less formal setting, delegates often could discuss more freely, exchange views, and find creative solutions to problems. This approach also promotes a more open and inclusive dialogue, allowing participants to share their ideas in a more spontaneous and collaborative way. As a result, informal discussions can often play an important role in building trusting relationships and building consensus on complex issues.

5.8.2.2. Interactive Debates

In debates or interactive discussions that encourage exchange between participants, a seated intervention may be preferred. This posture makes it easier for the
representative to engage in exchanges, listen carefully to other stakeholders and
actively participate in the conversation. By being seated, the delegate can adopt a
more open and receptive attitude, thus promoting a constructive and collaborative
dialogue. In this way, participants can share their perspectives, express their concerns, and exchange ideas more fluidly. This approach also fosters an environment
conducive to problem-solving and the search for collaborative solutions.

5.8.2.3. Panels or Round Tables

During panels or round tables, where several speakers are present and discuss
a common topic, representatives can opt for a seated intervention. This posture
promotes better coordination with other participants and facilitates the exchange
of ideas in a collaborative manner. By being seated, speakers can interact more
easily with each other, share their points of view and answer questions posed
by the audience more fluidly. In addition, this approach allows participants to
focus on the content of the discussion rather than their physical posture, which
contributes to a more dynamic and enriching exchange. In short, the interventions
seated during panels or round tables offer a framework conducive to collaboration
and the creation of synergies between the various actors involved.

5.8.2.4. Technical or Detailed Presentations

When technical or detailed presentations are required, a seated intervention may
be more convenient. This posture allows the representative to have at his disposal
supports such as documents, graphics, or visual presentations, and to consult
them more easily while making his speech. While seated, the representative can
have access to a desk or table to arrange their documents in an organized manner,
making it easier to handle and reference during the presentation. Additionally,
this approach makes it easier for the audience to follow the complex information presented, as the rep can refer to the visuals in a more natural and intuitive
way. In summary, seated interventions are particularly suitable for technical or

detailed presentations, offering better accessibility and a more fluid presentation of information.

5.8.2.5. Questions and Answers

During multilateral meetings, there are situations where informality prevails, which can lead representatives to opt for seated interventions. In these contexts, the aim is to create a more relaxed atmosphere and to promote informal exchanges between participants. When discussions are less formal, representatives may choose to speak seated to give a more relaxed and friendly impression. This approach also helps to reduce barriers between participants and promote more open and spontaneous communication. By adopting a seated posture, reps can feel more comfortable sharing ideas, asking questions, and engaging in informal conversations with their peers. This helps to create an environment conducive to the exchange of information and the building of people-to-people relationships within multilateral forums.

5.8.2.6. Informality

At multilateral meetings, speaking seated can give a more relaxed and friendly feel, creating a more informal and supportive environment. In these contexts where informality prevails, representatives may choose to speak seated to encourage informal exchanges between participants. This approach aims to reduce social barriers and encourage more open and spontaneous communication.

One of the reasons why stakeholders opt for seated interventions at multilateral meetings is to create a more relaxed atmosphere. This atmosphere can facilitate exchanges by allowing participants to feel more comfortable sharing ideas, asking questions, and engaging in informal conversations with their peers. By adopting a seated posture, representatives can help build trust and camaraderie, which promotes more fluid and effective communication.

In addition, seated interventions can also allow for greater physical proximity between participants, which can strengthen interpersonal bonds and facilitate collaboration. When representatives are seated at the same table or in the same space, they have an easier opportunity to exchange ideas, share perspectives, and work together on common solutions.

In summary, sitting down at multilateral meetings can help to create a more relaxed and friendly environment for informal and constructive exchanges among participants. This approach promotes open and spontaneous communication, strengthens interpersonal relationships, and facilitates collaboration to find solutions to global challenges.

5.8.2.7. Informal Meetings

In informal meetings, participants are encouraged to express themselves freely and openly, without the formal constraints often associated with formal meetings. In this context, seated interventions are favored to create a friendly atmosphere and encourage relaxed participation.

These informal gatherings provide a space for the exchange of ideas and discussion without the rigid protocols that can sometimes hinder communication. By opting for seated interventions, participants help to create a relaxed atmosphere where everyone feels free to share their opinions and points of view.

This approach also helps foster more open and relaxed participation, where participants can interact more freely and develop ideas collaboratively. By sitting

Illustration of an Informal Meeting Between Members of CARICOM Member Countries in Antigua and Barbuda

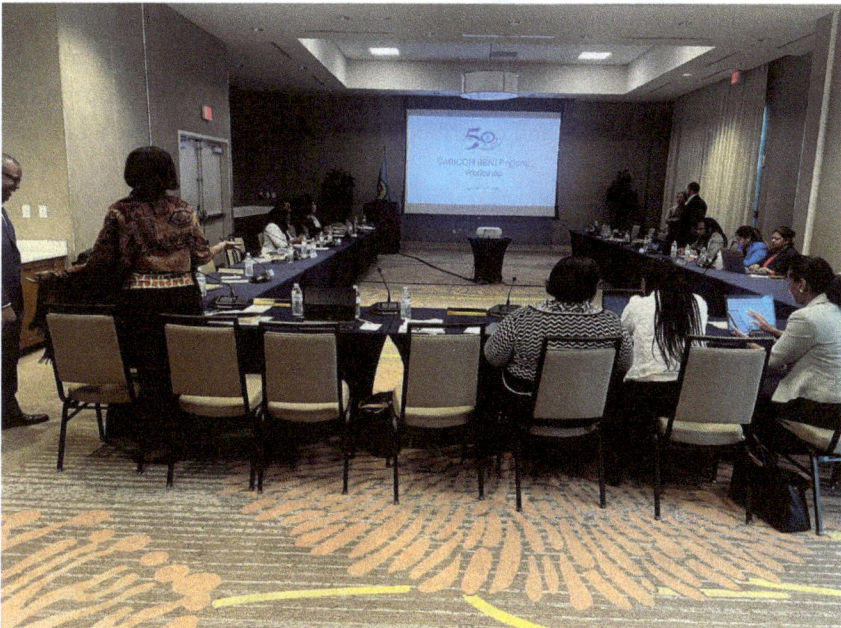

around a table or in an informal environment, representatives can build closer personal and professional relationships, which can strengthen relationships and foster better mutual understanding.

In summary, informal meetings promote more fluid communication and open participation, and seated interventions are an effective way to create a friendly and relaxed atmosphere. These meetings provide a valuable space for dialogue and collaboration among participants, helping to strengthen relationships and promote fruitful exchanges.

5.8.2.8. Collaborative Atmosphere

When the atmosphere is informal at multilateral meetings, it promotes a collaborative approach where representatives see themselves as equal partners rather than official actors. This collaborative atmosphere creates a more open space for discussion, where everyone can contribute in an equitable and informal way, without the formal constraints of standing interventions.

In this context, participants feel more comfortable expressing their ideas and points of view, which promotes a dynamic of collaboration and exchange. By seeing each other as equal partners, representatives are more likely to work together to find common solutions and advance discussions.

This collaborative approach also encourages a spirit of openness and flexibility, where ideas can be freely exchanged and discussed. Participants are thus encouraged to share their experiences and knowledge in a spirit of cooperation, which enriches the debates and contributes to the search for creative and innovative solutions.

In short, a collaborative atmosphere fosters more active and engaged participation of representatives in multilateral meetings, leading to more productive exchanges and the search for concerted solutions to global challenges.

5.8.2.9. Dynamic Interaction

Where multilateral meetings are designed to encourage interaction and dialogue among participants, seated interventions allow for greater flexibility in exchanges. Representatives can focus on listening to other stakeholders, asking questions, or engaging in more spontaneous and fluid discussions.

This dynamic interaction fosters an open and constructive dialogue, where ideas can be exchanged in a fluid and informal way. Participants are encouraged to share their perspectives and experiences, which enriches the discussions and contributes to a better mutual understanding of the issues.

In addition, this approach fosters a climate of trust and collaboration among participants, which can facilitate consensus-building and collaborative decision-making. By encouraging active and engaged participation of all actors, dynamic interaction maximizes the impact of multilateral meetings and promotes effective cooperation to address global challenges.

5.8.2.10. Promoting the Participation of All

Informality and seated interventions can help break down hierarchical barriers and encourage greater participation of all actors. This allows representatives of countries or organizations of all sizes to speak freely and contribute equitably to the discussions.

By fostering a more casual and inclusive discussion environment, multilateral meetings can give everyone the opportunity to make their voices heard and share their perspectives. Seated interventions create a sense of equality among participants, which encourages active and engaged participation by all.

This approach helps to strengthen the legitimacy and credibility of decisions taken at multilateral meetings, ensuring that all voices are heard and considered. It also fosters the creation of a broader consensus and a better mutual understanding of the issues, which can lead to more effective and sustainable solutions to global problems.

5.8.2.11. Creating a More Open Environment

Where multilateral meetings aim to foster open and honest exchanges, seated interventions create an environment where representatives can feel more comfortable sharing their ideas and concerns. This promotes more direct and informal communication, allowing for more frank and constructive discussions.

It is important to note that informality and seated interventions are not always appropriate in all contexts. Multilateral meetings can vary considerably in terms of protocol, the nature of the discussions, and the standards observed. Decisions about whether to speak seated or standing, therefore, depend on the specific setting of each meeting and the objectives sought by the representatives.

5.8.2.12. Comfort and Stability

In addition to the informal aspect, seated interventions at multilateral meetings also offer advantages in terms of comfort and stability.

First, sitting can provide more physical comfort to reps, allowing them to focus more on the content of their speech rather than their posture or balance. This physical stability can promote better articulation of ideas and more fluid communication.

Additionally, sitting creates a more relaxed environment, which can reduce the stress and anxiety associated with public speaking. Representatives may feel more comfortable expressing their opinions and participating in discussions more openly and authentically.

Finally, the convenience of comfort and stability offered by seated interventions allows representatives to fully focus on the issues and debates at hand, without being distracted by concerns related to their physical position. This promotes more active and engaged participation in multilateral discussions, contributing to more productive exchanges and more meaningful outcomes.

5.8.2.13. Physical Comfort

Multilateral meetings can often be long-term events, involving many hours of discussion and deliberation. Doing a seated intervention allows representatives to feel more comfortable physically, avoiding the fatigue associated with prolonged standing. This allows them to focus more on the content of their speech and maintain better clarity of mind. By avoiding the physical discomforts associated with standing, representatives can also be more receptive to ongoing discussions and participate more engaged in debates, contributing to more productive exchanges and more meaningful outcomes.

5.8.2.14. Emotional Stability

Seated interventions can help create an atmosphere of emotional stability for representatives. By sitting, they may feel more grounded and grounded, which can help them stay calm and focused during their procedure. It can also help them manage stress and emotions that can arise during intense or sensitive discussions.

5.8.2.15. Access to Documents and Media

When a representative wants to refer to documents, reports, or other visual aids during their speech, being seated makes it easier to access these resources. They can consult them more easily on a table or lectern, without having to juggle documents while standing. This allows for a smoother and more structured presentation.

5.8.2.16. Technical Precision

Some interventions at multilateral meetings may require technical clarification or detailed explanations. Being seated provides the opportunity to take notes or refer to specific information, which can help the rep provide more accurate and complete details during their speech.

5.8.2.17. Physical Balance

Some people may have health problems or mobility issues that make them more comfortable when sitting. In these cases, opting for a seated intervention helps to ensure their comfort and physical well-being during multilateral meetings.

It is important to note that the choice between sitting or standing depends on individual preferences, the specific context of the meeting and the standards observed. The comfort and stability provided by seated interventions can contribute to better representative performance and promote more effective communication at multilateral meetings.

5.8.2.18. Interaction with Colleagues

During some discussions or debates, it may be more convenient to be seated to facilitate interaction with colleagues and actively participate in exchanges.

Interaction with colleagues is an important aspect of multilateral meetings, and how representatives choose to speak, whether seated or standing, can influence this interaction. Here we highlight a few key points to develop this subject.

5.8.2.19. Collaboration and Informal Exchanges

When representatives are seated, they are more easily accessible to other partici-pants, which promotes informal exchanges and collaboration among colleagues. They can reach out to their neighbors, engage in more spontaneous conversations, and share ideas more informally, which helps to strengthen relationships and foster cooperation. This physical proximity also encourages the creation of informal networks, where representatives can exchange information outside of official sessions, thus strengthening mutual understanding and trust among participants. These informal interactions are often crucial for the development of strategic partnerships and alliances, which can influence discussions and decisions taken at multilateral meetings.

5.8.2.20. Linkage

Multilateral meetings often provide an opportunity for representatives of dif-ferent countries or organizations to meet and establish professional ties. When seated, reps can more easily engage in conversations, introduce themselves to each other, and make personal contacts, which can lead to future collabora-tions. These informal interactions are essential for building strong professional networks, strengthening international cooperation, and fostering the develop-ment of lasting diplomatic relations. By connecting with other representatives, participants can also access resources, information, and opportunities for col-laboration that can be beneficial to their respective countries or organizations. Thus, multilateral meetings serve not only as a platform for formal discussions but also as a framework for the development of important interpersonal and professional relationships.

5.8.2.21. Cooperation and Coordination

During meetings, representatives may be required to work in groups or coordinate their positions with other colleagues. Being seated allows them to physically get closer to their colleagues, share information, discuss strategies, and make joint decisions in a more convenient and efficient way. This physical proximity promotes more direct and spontaneous communication, making it easier to solve problems and make quick decisions when needed. In addition, sitting around a table allows participants to visualize working relationships and reinforce a sense of belonging to a group or team. By working closely together, representatives can better understand each other's concerns and interests, which promotes cooperation and coordination of actions to achieve common goals.

5.8.2.22. Reactions and Mutual Support

When a rep speaks, colleagues sitting nearby can react in real time, offering signs of support, approval, or disagreement. This creates a more dynamic interaction climate, where reps can feel supported by their colleagues and benefit from immediate feedback, which can influence their speech and positioning. This group dynamic also fosters the emergence of informal coalitions among like-minded representatives, strengthening their ability to promote their common interests and influence decisions taken at multilateral meetings.

5.8.2.23. Professional Networking

Multilateral meetings are also opportunities for professional networking, where representatives can network with key players in the field. Being seated facilitates informal conversations on the sidelines of formal meetings, allowing representatives to connect with other professionals, exchange ideas, and discuss possible future collaborations.

It is important to note that interaction with colleagues can also occur during standing interventions, especially during formal debates or Q&A. However, sitting can foster more continuous and informal interaction throughout multilateral meetings, thereby strengthening professional ties and facilitating cooperation between representatives.

It is important to note that the decision to sit or stand also depends on the norms and customs observed at UN General Assembly meetings. It can be helpful to observe the common practices of other stakeholders and to consider cultural and protocol expectations when making decisions. Regardless of the position chosen, it is essential to focus on the clarity, impact, and relevance of the speech to effectively convey its message to the audience.

5.9. Standing from the Main Stand

The intervention from the main gallery at multilateral meetings is a particularly significant moment. It provides an opportunity for representatives of countries or organizations to make their voices heard in front of a wider international audience. This main forum is usually the place where official speeches, policy statements, and important announcements are made.

When a speaker speaks from the main gallery, several reading materials may be used. Some of the most common include paper, tablets, laptops or desktops, and even printed text. However, the use of a teleprompter is also becoming more widespread, especially when it comes to long or formal speeches.

The teleprompter is a device that displays the text of the speech invisibly to the audience, usually on a screen placed in front of the speaker. This device allows the speaker to read his speech while maintaining eye contact with the audience. This can be especially useful for complex speeches or official statements where every word counts.

A Speech Standing from the Main Rostrum
of the United Nations General Assembly

When speaking from the main gallery, the speaker must not only master his speech but also captivate the audience and convey his message convincingly. It is essential to maintain clear and concise language, use relevant examples to illustrate your points, and structure the speech in a logical way.

The choice of reading medium will often depend on the speaker's personal preferences, the nature of the speech, and the availability of equipment. Some speakers prefer to have a hard copy of their speech for last-minute annotations, while others opt for the simplicity of a teleprompter. Regardless of the medium chosen, the key to success lies in careful preparation, in-depth knowledge of the subject, and the ability to communicate convincingly.

In conclusion, speaking from the main podium at multilateral meetings is an opportunity to share important messages with an international audience. The choice of reading medium, whether it is paper, tablet, computer, or teleprompter, will depend on the needs of the speaker and the circumstances. Regardless of the medium used, the key is to communicate effectively to influence international public opinion and contribute to debates on global issues.

5.9.1. Teleprompter Intervention

Using a teleprompter during a speech can add a touch of professionalism and fluidity to a speech. However, it is true that spectators, including colleagues in the room, are not always aware of its use. This can give the impression that the speaker is delivering his or her speech in a fluid and natural way, without the need for written support.

During my first experience with a teleprompter, I was surprised by the positive reaction of my audience. Several colleagues came to congratulate me for giving an excellent speech without the help of a paper medium. This demonstrates how discreet and effective the use of the teleprompter can be.

It is important to note that the teleprompter displays the text in a manner that is synchronized with the speaker's rate. This means that if the speaker slows down, the text scrolls more slowly, and if it pauses, the teleprompter also stops. This feature allows the speaker to maintain constant eye contact with the audience, turning their gaze left and right to address the entire audience.

In summary, the use of a teleprompter can be a valuable tool for speakers at multilateral meetings, providing an elegant way to deliver a speech while maintaining eye contact with the audience. It is essential to practice using it effectively to ensure a successful presentation.

Image of the Teleprompter Booth at the General Assembly

5.9.1.1. Procedure for Requesting the Teleprompter

Some speakers prefer to use a teleprompter when presenting their speech. The request for the use of a teleprompter or similar visual aids at the UN or at multilateral meetings must follow a specific process to ensure that the response runs smoothly. In most multilateral forums, the teleprompter is available to all delegates or all persons who are to speak in the official forum such as the UN General Assembly. Here is a general procedure to follow:

Advance Preparation: Before applying, make sure that you have prepared the text of your speech or intervention professionally. The text must be clear, concise, and adapted to the teleprompter format.

Identification of the Need: Determine if you really need a teleprompter or other visual aids. Teleprompters are useful for long speeches or complex interventions. If your speech is relatively short and simple, it may be more effective to memorize it or have it in the form of notes.

Contact with the Host Organization: If you are attending a meeting or conference organized by the UN or another multilateral organization, contact the event organizers or organizers for specific procedures. They will be able to tell you if it is possible to use a teleprompter and how to apply.

Formal Request: Submit a formal request for the use of the teleprompter, following the instructions provided by the host organization. This request should include details such as the date and time of your intervention, the room where it will take place, and information about the text you want to display on the teleprompter.

Collaborate with Technicians: Once your request is accepted, work closely with the organization's technicians to ensure that the teleprompter is set up correctly and that the text is displayed as expected. Allow enough time for testing and adjustments before the actual operation.

Rehearsal: Rehearse your speech repeatedly using the teleprompter to familiarize yourself with how it works. The fluency of your speech will depend on your ability to follow the text displayed.

Careful Use: When intervening, use the teleprompter with care. Keep eye contact with your audience as much as possible, while occasionally glancing at the teleprompter to guide you.

Have a Plan B: In the event of a technical problem with the teleprompter, always have a backup plan, such as paper notes, to avoid interruptions.

Acknowledgements: At the end of your talk, thank the host organization for setting up the teleprompter and make sure the text is properly erased for subsequent speakers.

Each multilateral organization may have its own specific procedures and requirements when it comes to teleprompter use, so it is essential to follow their instructions and communicate with their technical teams for effective coordination.

5.9.2. Visual Impact

By standing, the representative can be more visible and attract more attention from the audience, especially in large rooms.

Indeed, visual impact is another important element of standing statements at multilateral meetings. Below are some more examples to illustrate how visual impact can play a significant role:

5.9.3. Speech to a Large Assembly

When the representative is addressing a large assembly, standing creates a stronger visual impact. This makes it easier for the rep to be spotted and capture the audience's attention.

5.9.4. Media Dissemination

Multilateral meetings are often widely publicized, with cameras recording and broadcasting speeches. Standing during a statement can improve the representative's visibility on screen, making their speech more impactful for the audience watching it on TV or online.

5.9.5. Symbolism

The standing posture can also take on a particular symbolism at certain multilateral meetings. For example, a representative may choose to stand to express a strong commitment to a specific cause, mark a moment of solidarity, or show respect for an important event or person.

5.9.6. Contrast with Other Interventions

If other participants are speaking seated, standing can create a visual contrast that will further enhance the representative's intervention. This can help to strengthen the impact and memorability of his speech.

5.9.7. Gestures and Body Expressions

Standing also provides more freedom to use gestures and body expressions that can enrich the representative's communication. These movements can be more visible and help reinforce the message and overall impact of the declaration.

By using the standing posture, representatives can leverage the visual impact to attract attention, strengthen their presence on stage, and improve the communication of their message at multilateral meetings.

5.9.8. Dynamic Styling

Some speakers prefer to speak standing up to feel more dynamic and energetic, which can enhance the impact of their speech. Indeed, the choice to make a standing statement at multilateral meetings can also be motivated by the desire to create a dynamic and energetic style. Let us consider these few more examples to illustrate how dynamic style can be strengthened:

5.9.9. Inspirational Speech

When a rep wants to convey an inspiring and motivating message, standing up can enhance the momentum and energy of their performance. This allows them to project a more dynamic presence and engage the audience more. By adopting this posture, the representative can captivate their audience, generate enthusiasm, and stimulate participant engagement. Standing speech is often associated with solemn or memorable moments, and it can be used successfully to galvanize minds and mobilize collective efforts around a common cause or goal.

5.9.10. Calls to Action

If the rep wants to inspire the audience to act or respond to a specific challenge, the standing posture can add strength and conviction to their calls to action. By standing up, the representative can project an image of determination and commitment, which reinforces the credibility of their calls and encourages participants to respond to their requests. This position often symbolizes a decisive moment when concrete measures are needed, and it can help create an atmosphere of urgency and mobilization around the proposed actions.

5.9.11. Visual Presentations

When a representative stands during a visual presentation, they are able to interact more directly with visual aids such as screens, charts, or graphs. This posture allows him to physically get closer to the visual aids, which facilitates the interaction and manipulation of these elements during his speech.

By standing, the representative can use broader and more expressive gestures to accompany his explanations and demonstrations. For example, they can point to certain elements on a graph, draw lines or arrows to highlight trends or correlations, or make hand gestures to illustrate abstract concepts. These dynamic gestures add vibrancy to the visual presentation and help to captivate the audience's attention.

In addition, the standing posture allows the representative to better control his body and gestures, which gives him greater ease and a better presence on stage. This builds the speaker's credibility and authority, which can help to further convince the audience of the validity of their arguments.

In summary, standing during a visual presentation allows the representative to interact more dynamically with visual aids, add expressive gestures to better illustrate their words, and reinforce their presence and authority on stage. This helps to make the presentation more engaging and effective for the audience.

5.9.12. Energetic Tone

When a representative stands to speak, it gives them a more dominant position and a more commanding physical presence. This natural posture often prompts the speaker to adopt a louder and more dynamic tone of voice. The simple act of standing up can inject a dose of energy into his voice, allowing him to project his voice with more power and conviction.

Additionally, standing promotes better blood circulation and deeper breathing, which can help strengthen the rep's vocal resonance. It is also easier for the speaker to move around and use larger, more expressive gestures to accompany their speech. These gestures, combined with an energetic tone of voice, help convey the speaker's emotion and engagement more effectively.

The energy and passion expressed through tone of voice can play a crucial role in keeping the audience's attention. A monotonous or dull speech can quickly lose the audience's interest, while an energetic and passionate tone can captivate and generate enthusiasm. In this way, the standing posture promotes more dynamic and engaging communication, allowing the representative to convey his message with more impact and efficiency.

5.9.13. Audience Interactions

The standing posture also facilitates direct interactions with the audience. The representative can move around the stage, get closer to the attendees, or make more direct eye contact, which can increase engagement and interaction with the audience.

By using the standing posture, reps can create extra momentum and energy in their speech, which can have a greater impact on the audience. This can be particularly effective when there is a need to generate enthusiasm, motivation, or action on the part of participants in multilateral meetings.

5.10. Leadership and Diplomacy in Multilateral Communication

Leadership and diplomacy are two closely related concepts, especially in the context of multilateral diplomatic communication. In international arenas, the way a country exercises leadership can have a direct impact on the dynamics of negotiations, strategic alliances, and the outcome of multilateral discussions.

Leadership in multilateral diplomacy is demonstrated by the ability of a State or its representative to guide debates, propose innovative solutions, and build consensus around these solutions. An effective leader in this context must be able to navigate the divergent interests of the different actors present, while maintaining a clear vision of his or her own country's objectives. Diplomatic leadership requires not only great expertise in foreign policy but also a mastery of communication techniques that allow one to persuade, influence, and unite others around a common cause.

As shown in Table 5, different leadership styles are applied in diplomacy depending on context, with notable examples from recent international figure.

Table 5: Diplomacy and Leadership

Leadership Style	Description	Application in Diplomacy	Examples of Diplomatic Leaders
Transformational Leadership	Inspire and motivate others to achieve a collective vision	Creating ambitious international agreements	Nelson Mandela, Kofi Annan
Transactional Leadership	Focuses on structured tasks, rewards, and clear responsibilities	Practical negotiations, trade agreements	Angela Merkel, Barack Obama
Situational Leadership	Adapt the leadership style according to the needs of the situation	Varies by crisis or collaboration	Winston Churchill during World War II

Diplomatic communication, as a tool of leadership, plays a crucial role in how a country projects its image and defends its interests on the international stage. It is used to clarify positions, express reservations, or propose compromises. A diplomatic leader must know how to use communication to build credibility, gain the trust of other actors, and navigate the complexities of multilateral negotiations. He must also be sensitive to the cultural and political nuances that influence the reception of diplomatic messages.

In multilateral negotiations, the relationship between leadership and diplomacy becomes particularly evident. Diplomats in leadership positions often have to act as mediators or facilitators, seeking to harmonize divergent positions while protecting the interests of their own nation. This role requires not only technical diplomatic skills but also an ability to inspire trust and build strategic alliances. A leader's ability to read power dynamics, anticipate the reactions of other States, and adjust strategy accordingly is essential to effectively navigating the often turbulent waters of multilateral diplomacy.

Leadership in multilateral diplomacy, therefore, is not simply a matter of the position or rank of a representative. It is the ability to influence decision-making

Receiving an Award by Wisnique Panier (Left)
at a Symposium on Diplomacy and Leadership

processes, build strong coalitions, and steer discussions toward outcomes that are both fair and beneficial to all parties involved. In this context, diplomatic communication becomes not only a means of expression but also a first-rate strategic tool to exercise leadership and guide international negotiations toward constructive and lasting solutions.

CHAPTER 6

Challenges and Solutions at Multilateral Meetings

Multilateral diplomacy is a complex arena where diplomatic representatives face a multitude of challenges, ranging from diverse viewpoints to deep disagreements and sensitive issues. This section explores the challenges inherent in multilateral meetings and offers practical solutions to address them successfully. By addressing these challenges, accompanied by concrete examples, this section aims to help diplomats anticipate, manage and overcome obstacles to international cooperation and common solutions. To this end, this chapter discusses the common challenges that diplomatic representatives face in multilateral meetings, as well as practical solutions to overcome them.

6.1. Language and Cultural Barriers

Multilateral meetings bring together delegates from diverse linguistic and cultural backgrounds, creating a complex environment where language and cultural barriers can become major challenges. The language barrier is one of the most obvious challenges in multilateral meetings, where more than one official language may be used. Delegates must ensure that their messages are understood by all. However, a deep understanding of these barriers and the implementation of appropriate strategies can turn these obstacles into opportunities to strengthen international cooperation. *The Language of Negotiation: A Handbook of Practical Strategies for Improving Communication* by Mulholland (1991) is also a reference work. This book looks at the language and communication skills needed to succeed in diplomacy and international negotiations. It offers practical advice to improve diplomatic communication.

Indeed, language and cultural barriers can make communication and understanding difficult at multilateral meetings. To overcome these challenges, it is important to promote the use of a common working language, such as English, and to provide professional interpreting services. Awareness and respect for cultural differences also promote effective communication and constructive dialogue.

For delegates whose mother tongue is not one of the working languages, the language barrier can be a challenge. For example, a bad translation can lead to misunderstandings. Some authors like Ringe (2022) show that multilingualism is common in world politics, especially in negotiations between politicians of different mother tongues. Nils Ringe analyzes the EU to show how it reduces the political nature of decisions. The use of foreign languages and translation promote simple and neutral communication, minimizing disagreements.

6.2. Interpretation and Language of Work

International organizations usually provide interpretation services to facilitate communication among delegates. Relying on these services is essential to ensure that each participant can express themselves and understand others. Fluency in one or more working languages, such as English, French, or Spanish, is an asset. Delegates may also use less common, but widely understood, languages to promote understanding. For example, during international climate negotiations, a delegate using Spanish may opt for English as the working language to ensure that their message reaches a wider audience.

6.3. Cultural Barrier

Cultural differences can lead to misunderstandings and conflicts. Delegates must be culturally sensitive to avoid unintentionally offending their counterparts. Delegates should take the time to study the culture and customs of other delegations to better understand their perspectives. Intercultural training can be useful.

6.4. Respectful Communication

Using respectful language, avoiding cultural stereotypes, and showing interest in other cultures help strengthen intercultural relations. For example, during trade negotiations, a Western delegate may recognize the importance of gift exchange in some Asian cultures by offering a small gift at official meetings.

In conclusion, language and cultural barriers should not be insurmountable obstacles in multilateral meetings. By taking a proactive and respectful approach, delegates can turn these challenges into opportunities to strengthen mutual understanding, cooperation, and the search for common solutions to global problems.

6.5. Complexity of the Issues

Multilateral meetings often take place in a context where complex global issues are discussed, ranging from peace and security to the economy, the environment and human rights. They often address complex and interconnected issues. To deal with them, it is essential to deepen your knowledge of the topics on the agenda, conduct thorough research, and consult with experts in the field. Working with other delegates and finding creative solutions can help solve complex problems and move toward mutually beneficial agreements.

A diplomat said:

> *The main challenges we face are often related to the diversity of interests and priorities of the different participating countries. It can be difficult to find common ground when positions are far apart. In addition, negotiations can sometimes be slowed down by complex bureaucratic processes and political rivalries between major powers.*

6.5.1. Interconnectedness of Issues

The interconnectedness of issues is an unavoidable reality in the context of multilateral meetings. Global issues are not limited to siloed areas but are often closely interconnected. This means that a decision or policy made in a particular area can have a significant impact on other aspects of global life.

Let us take a concrete example to illustrate this interconnection of issues: economic policies. The economic decisions made by a country, such as interest rates, tax policies or trade agreements, have consequences that go far beyond the economic realm. They can influence food security by affecting the availability of financial resources for agriculture, as well as access to global markets for food products. Moreover, these economic decisions can also impact energy issues by influencing investments in renewable energy or fossil fuels.

This interconnectedness of issues creates a complex web of issues where decisions made in one area can have unexpected repercussions in other areas. This underlines the importance of considering the cross-cutting implications of any policy or decision in multilateral meetings.

To address this reality, it is essential that participants in multilateral meetings adopt a holistic approach and consider the linkages between different issues. This requires a thorough analysis of the potential consequences of each decision and coordination between the different stakeholders to minimize negative effects and maximize positive synergies.

Ultimately, the interconnectedness of issues makes multilateral meetings even more crucial, as they provide a forum for actors from around the world to collaborate on complex and interrelated challenges. A thorough understanding of these interconnections is essential.

6.5.2. Diversity of Actors

The diversity of actors in multilateral meetings is one of their most important characteristics. These events bring together a multitude of actors, ranging from nation-states to non-governmental organizations (NGOs), the private sector, UN agencies, civil society groups, academic experts, and many others. Each of these actors brings their own perspective, interests, and objectives, creating a complex dynamic within multilateral negotiations.

This diversity of actors is both a strength and a challenge. On the one hand, it allows for a diverse range of perspectives and expertise to be considered, which can enrich debates and promote more comprehensive and balanced solutions. NGOs, for example, often bring perspectives based on field experience and play a crucial role in raising awareness on human rights, sustainable development, and humanitarian aid issues.

On the other hand, the diversity of actors can also make consensus-building more difficult. Competing interests, national priorities, and hidden agendas can complicate negotiations and lead to deadlocks. Sometimes, powerful States or special interest groups can exert disproportionate influence, which can create imbalances in the outcome of the negotiations.

To overcome these challenges, the organizers of multilateral meetings must create mechanisms and spaces for all actors to participate in an equitable and transparent manner. This may include pre-consultations, thematic working groups, civil society forums, and other initiatives to foster open and inclusive dialogue.

Ultimately, diversity of actors is an unavoidable reality in multilateral meetings, and it reflects the complexity of today's global issues. Managing this diversity constructively is essential to move toward solutions that address the needs and concerns of the entire international community.

6.5.3. Evolving Challenges

The ever-changing global challenges are a fundamental feature of multilateral meetings. These challenges are evolving for a variety of reasons, including rapid technological developments, the emergence of unforeseen crises, and changes in global public opinion. This changing dynamic requires great flexibility and responsiveness on the part of diplomats and actors involved in these forums.

Technological advancement is one of the main driving forces behind the evolution of global challenges. New technologies[1] create new opportunities, but they also bring their own set of challenges. For example, the rise of the internet and social media has radically transformed the way information is disseminated and how public opinion is formed. This can have a significant impact on diplomacy by quickly exposing actions or policies to a global audience and creating pressures for immediate responses.

Unforeseen crises, such as major natural disasters, sudden conflicts, or global health crises, can also disrupt the agenda of multilateral meetings. Responding to such crises often requires rapid and effective coordination between nations and international organizations, which tests the ability of diplomats to adapt quickly to new realities.

In addition, changes in global public opinion can influence the priorities and objectives of multilateral meetings. Social movements, awareness campaigns, and pressure from civil society can lead governments and international organizations to reassess their positions and take action to address popular concerns.

In response to these constant developments, diplomats must be prepared to adjust their approaches and strategies in response to changing circumstances. This requires effective communication, the ability to adapt quickly and a willingness to seek creative solutions to new challenges as they arise. Multilateral meetings play a critical role in providing a forum for international actors to work together to address emerging and evolving issues affecting our world.

---

[1] With the rise of new technologies and digital diplomacy, States must adapt their communication strategies to remain influential on the international stage.

6.6. Solutions to Manage Complexity

Whether it is complex trade negotiations, regional conflicts, global climate change or international security issues, diplomatic actors, whether States, international organizations, or individuals, are faced with the need to navigate this complex landscape to achieve their goals.

In this section, we will discuss topics such as managing complexity in international negotiations, creating and maintaining strategic alliances, coordinating international efforts to solve global problems, and managing conflicts. We will highlight case studies and real-world examples to illustrate these concepts.

Managing complexity is a crucial skill in diplomacy and international relations, as it allows us to deal with multifaceted and constantly evolving problems. Whether you are a seasoned diplomat or a student of international relations, this section will provide you with insights and strategies to successfully address the complex challenges of today's world.

6.6.1. Holistic Approach

Diplomats need to take a holistic approach by looking at issues from all angles. This means considering the interconnections between issues and long-term implications. The holistic approach, in the context of diplomacy and international relations, is one that recognizes the interdependence and complexity of global problems. Rather than dealing with issues in a fragmented and isolated manner, a holistic approach seeks to understand the connections and interactions between different aspects of international affairs.

This approach considers that global problems cannot be solved in isolation, as they are often interconnected. For example, security issues may be related to economic issues, ethnic conflicts, or environmental issues. A holistic approach examines how these factors interact and how they influence international dynamics.

The holistic approach also emphasizes international cooperation. It recognizes that global problems often require collective action and that multilateral diplomacy is an effective tool to address these problems. It encourages coordination among States, international organizations, non-State actors, and civil society to develop comprehensive solutions.

In summary, the holistic approach to diplomacy and international relations emphasizes understanding the complexity of global issues, finding connections between these issues, and promoting international cooperation to solve these problems in a comprehensive manner. It recognizes that today's world is inter-connected and that effective solutions require a holistic view.

6.6.2. Multilateral Collaboration

Multilateral meetings are designed to encourage cooperation among stakeholders. Diplomats need to foster dialogue and coalition-building to address complex issues. Multilateral collaboration, also known as multilateral cooperation, is a fundamental principle of international relations that involves the participation of multiple actors, such as States, international organizations, non-State actors, and civil society, to solve complex global or regional problems. This form of cooperation is based on dialogue, negotiation, and the search for common solutions to address challenges that transcend national borders.

Multilateral collaboration often takes the form of international agreements, treaties, or conventions to which several countries are signatories. It can also manifest itself in joint initiatives to address issues such as climate change, global security, public health, international trade, human rights, and many other areas.

One of the most emblematic examples of multilateral collaboration is the UN, which brings together Member States from around the world to promote peace, security, sustainable development, and human rights globally. UN specialized agencies, such as the World Health Organization (WHO) and the United Nations Environment Program (UNEP), also work in collaboration with member countries to address specific issues.

6.6.3. Innovation and Adaptability

In the face of ever-changing problems, diplomats must be open to innovation and ready to adapt their approaches. This may include exploring new technologies or new funding mechanisms. The Paris Climate Agreement is an example of a response to the complexity of global environmental issues. It aims to address the climate crisis by mobilizing extensive multilateral cooperation, recognizing the interconnectedness between greenhouse gas emissions, energy policy, and sustainable development.

Ultimately, the complexity of the issues in multilateral forums is not only a challenge but also an opportunity to find innovative solutions and take concerted action on the world's most pressing issues. Diplomats who understand the complex nature of these issues are better equipped to promote international cooperation and shape a more sustainable future.

6.7. Differences of Opinion and Positions

Multilateral meetings bring together delegates from different nations and organizations, each bringing their own interests, priorities, and perspectives. Thus,
differences of opinion and positions between delegates can lead to tensions and
blockages at multilateral meetings. These differences of opinion and positions
are inevitable, but the way they are handled can make the difference between
deadlock and fruitful cooperation. It is important to maintain an open mind, listen
carefully to different perspectives, and look for commonalities and compromise
solutions. From this perspective, diplomacy is often about finding common ground
and working together despite differences. This section explores the challenges
posed by these discrepancies and proposes strategies to overcome them.

6.7.1. National Interests

The pursuit of national interests is an essential element of multilateral meetings.
States participate in these forums to defend and promote their national interests,
whether economic, political, environmental, or security issues. However, this
pursuit of national interests can often lead to disagreements on how to deal with
certain issues.

Each State has its own priorities and concerns, and these priorities can sometimes conflict with those of other States. For example, in international trade,
one State may seek to protect its domestic industry by imposing tariff barriers,
while another State may insist on greater openness and freer access to markets.
Such disagreements over trade policies can impede multilateral negotiations to
conclude trade agreements.

Similarly, disagreements on environmental issues are frequent. Some States
may have economies that are heavily dependent on extractive industries, while
others may favor strict environmental policies. This can lead to confrontations
over how to manage natural resources in a sustainable way.

Disagreements over international security are also common. States may have
differing views on how to resolve regional conflicts, combat terrorism, or prevent
the proliferation of nuclear weapons. These disagreements can hinder efforts to
achieve peaceful solutions and conflict resolution.

However, despite these potential disagreements, multilateral meetings provide
a critical forum for States to discuss their national interests, seek compromises,
and work together to solve global problems. Multilateral diplomacy often requires

complex negotiations and compromises to reach agreements acceptable to all participating States. It also requires the ability to set aside short-term national interests in favor of long-term common goals, such as global peace, security, and stability.

6.7.2. Ideologies and Values

Multilateral meetings bring together delegations from countries with various political, cultural, and ideological systems. These ideological and value differences between delegations can lead to disagreements on various issues, including human rights, democracy, and social justice.

For example, some delegations may promote democratic values and insist on respect for human rights as essential foundations of global peace and stability. They can advocate for democracy, freedom of expression and the protection of minorities as universal principles that should be respected by all States.

However, other delegations may have different perspectives on governance and human rights. They can emphasize national sovereignty and support authoritarian models of governance. These delegations may consider that democratic standards and human rights should be determined by each country according to its own history, culture, and specific values.

Such ideological and value disagreements can complicate multilateral negotiations, especially when it comes to sensitive issues such as international sanctions, military interventions, or investigations into human rights violations. Deep differences of opinion on these issues can make it difficult to reach consensus in multilateral forums.

However, multilateral diplomacy also provides a space for dialogue and debate on these issues. Multilateral meetings provide a platform where delegations can express their views, discuss their differences and seek constructive solutions. While ideological and value disagreements may persist, these forums allow international actors to work together on other issues where consensus is possible, thus contributing to the resolution of global problems.

6.7.3. Policy Priorities

Multilateral meetings bring together governments with varying political priorities, which can lead to disagreements over what to do. Each State pursues its own national goals and interests, and these political priorities may conflict with those of other States.

For example, in multilateral trade negotiations, some countries may prioritize the protection of their domestic industry and the promotion of their exports, while others may seek to further open their markets and boost international trade. These divergent priorities can make it difficult to reach balanced trade agreements.

Similarly, when discussing environmental issues, countries may have different policy priorities depending on their own needs and concerns. Some States may insist on reducing greenhouse gas emissions to combat climate change, while others may highlight the need to protect their industrial sector and jobs. These divergences in political priorities can complicate negotiations on multilateral environmental agreements.

However, multilateral diplomacy aims to find compromises between these divergent political priorities. Multilateral meetings provide a forum where States can discuss their differences, explore compromise solutions, and develop agreements that consider the interests of all stakeholders. While disagreements may persist, multilateral diplomacy allows governments to work together to solve complex global problems and achieve common goals, even when considering their different political priorities.

6.8. Solutions to Manage Discrepancies

Managing differences at multilateral meetings is a crucial skill in the diplomatic field. Multilateral meetings often bring together a variety of actors, from States to non-governmental organizations to the private sector, and the issues discussed can be complex and controversial. In this context, it is common for differences of opinion to arise, which can make it difficult to reach consensus. However, there are several solutions and approaches that can help resolve these disputes and reach mutually acceptable agreements.

The importance of managing differences lies in the fact that multilateral meetings often aim to resolve complex global problems such as international conflicts, humanitarian crises, and environmental and economic issues, among others. The stakes are high, and finding solutions is essential to advance the common interests of the international community.

In this section, we will explore various solutions and techniques for managing differences in multilateral meetings. These solutions range from the importance of open dialogue to neutral mediation, to the development of compromises and the search for common ground. Each of these approaches can play a crucial role in resolving differences and finding balanced solutions to global challenges.

It is important to note that managing differences is not only a diplomatic skill but also an essential skill in many areas of life, from family dispute resolution to international business negotiation. The skills we will explore here have a reach far beyond multilateral meetings and can be applied in many situations where differences of opinion must be overcome to reach constructive agreements.

6.8.1. Constructive Dialogue

Diplomats must encourage an open and constructive dialogue. Listening carefully to the arguments of other delegations and asking questions to better understand their positions can help to establish common ground. Thus, constructive dialogue is a communication approach that aims to resolve conflicts, promote mutual understanding, and reach positive solutions through discussions or negotiations. It is based on the principles of respect, open-mindedness, active listening, and the search for common ground. The goal of constructive dialogue is to reach a mutually beneficial consensus or resolution, avoiding unnecessary confrontations and escalations of conflicts. Key elements of constructive dialogue include:

1. *Active Listening*: Participants are encouraged to listen carefully to the perspectives of others, without interruptions or judgment. This creates an environment conducive to mutual understanding.
2. *Empathy*: Participants are encouraged to put themselves in each other's shoes and try to understand their feelings, concerns, and needs. This promotes empathy and compassion.
3. *Open and Honest Communication*: Constructive dialogue is based on transparency and honesty. Participants are encouraged to express their opinions and concerns in a clear and respectful manner.
4. *Seeking Common Solutions*: Rather than getting bogged down in opposing positions, constructive dialogue seeks to identify solutions that benefit all parties. It is a question of finding compromises that are acceptable to all.
5. *Emotional Management*: Emotions can run high when discussing sensitive topics. Constructive dialogue includes techniques for managing these emotions and maintaining a productive discussion climate.
6. *Peaceful Conflict Resolution*: The goal is to resolve conflicts peacefully, avoiding violence, personal attacks, or unnecessary escalations.

Constructive dialogue is particularly important in international relations, diplomacy, mediation, and conflict resolution. It can be used to address complex political, economic, social, or cultural issues. For example, during peace negotiations between nations in conflict, constructive dialogue can be essential to reach a lasting agreement.

In summary, constructive dialogue is an essential communication approach that promotes conflict resolution, mutual understanding, and cooperation. It is based on the principles of respect, empathy, and the search for common solutions to achieve positive results.

6.8.2. Trade-Off

Compromises are often necessary to make progress. Diplomats must seek intermediate solutions that consider the concerns of all parties. Compromise is a conflict resolution strategy that aims to reach an agreement that is acceptable to all parties involved. It is a process in which the dissenting parties are willing to make concessions to find a solution that, while perhaps different from their original positions, is acceptable and mutually beneficial. The search for compromise is a key element of diplomacy, negotiation, and conflict resolution, whether at the international, national, or individual level. Consider these few key principles of trade-off:

1. *Flexibility*: Parties must be willing to adapt and adjust their positions to find common ground. This often requires an open mind and a willingness to consider alternative solutions.
2. *Communication*: Open and honest communication is essential to understanding the needs and concerns of all parties. It is important to listen actively and to express yourself clearly and respectfully.
3. *Recognition of Common Interests*: Identifying shared interests or common goals can help find solutions that meet the needs of all parties. It is a question of looking for areas where interests converge.
4. *Prioritizing Issues*: It can be helpful to prioritize issues or points of disagreement based on their importance. This allows you to focus on the most crucial issues and find solutions for those first.
5. *Balanced Concessions*: Concessions must be made in a balanced manner so that each side is willing to give in on certain points while preserving its fundamental interests.

6. *Neutral Mediation*: In some situations, neutral mediation can make it easier to find compromises by helping the parties communicate constructively and explore resolution options.
7. *Mutual Respect*: Maintaining mutual respect throughout the process is essential to maintaining a positive bargaining climate.

Compromise is often used in contexts such as international politics, trade negotiations, family or professional disputes, and even in the resolution of personal disagreements. It is based on the notion that cooperation and the search for balanced solutions are often preferable to stalemate or protracted conflicts.

In summary, the search for compromise is a strategic approach aimed at reaching mutually acceptable agreements by making balanced concessions. It is based on the principles of flexibility, communication, the pursuit of common interests, and mutual respect. This approach is widely used to resolve a variety of conflicts at different levels.

6.8.3. Coalition Building

Creating alliances with delegations sharing similar interests can strengthen the position of a group of countries and help influence discussions. For example, during the negotiations on the UN Sustainable Development Goals, countries had to deal with differences of opinion on development priorities. However, through continuous dialogue and compromise, consensus was eventually reached on a set of ambitious goals.

The effective management of differences of opinion and positions in multilateral meetings is a key element of diplomacy. It requires patience, diplomacy, and a commitment to finding common solutions. Delegates who succeed in turning disagreements into opportunities for cooperation strengthen the capacity of multilateral meetings to address complex global challenges.

6.9. Strained Diplomatic Relations

Multilateral meetings are crucial arenas where representatives of the world's States come together to discuss and collaborate on global issues. However, sometimes these meetings take place against the backdrop of strained diplomatic relations between certain countries due to historical disagreements, ongoing conflicts, or other factors. In such situations, the proper management of these tensions is essential to preserve constructive dialogue and foster positive outcomes. In other words, the management of tense diplomatic relations in multilateral meetings remains and remains a major challenge for cooperation despite the frictions. This section briefly explores the challenges of strained diplomatic relations and presents strategies for addressing them. The book *A Critical Discourse Analysis of Iran and US Presidential Speeches at the UN: The Sociopragmatic Functions* (Najarzadegan et al. 2017) examines the critical analysis of diplomatic discourse by examining speech acts in selected Iranian and American presidential speeches related to the events of September 11 and the Iraq War. The author analyzes how language is used in these discourses to influence perceptions, international relations, and political decisions. The book offers a valuable perspective on the dimensions of diplomatic discourse in the context of these major conflicts.

6.9.1. Historical Conflicts

Some delegations may harbor deep resentments toward others because of past conflicts. Historical conflicts represent a complex and sometimes painful chapter in human history. These conflicts, often deeply rooted in the past, have left lasting scars on societies, nations, and individuals. They are the result of disagreements, rivalries, competitions, ideological differences, or territorial claims that have led to violent confrontations, wars, genocide, or other forms of violence.

Historical conflicts can have a variety of origins, ranging from ethnic, religious, or cultural tensions to political or economic conflicts. Some of these conflicts have had major global consequences, shaping global geopolitics and the global economy, while others have had a more localized, but equally significant, impact on the communities involved.

The study and understanding of historical conflicts is essential for several reasons. First, they allow for the analysis of the causes and consequences of these conflicts, which can inform decisions made by current and future generations. Second, they offer valuable lessons about conflict resolution mechanisms, showing what has worked and what has not worked in the past. Finally, they stress the need to promote reconciliation, justice and intercultural understanding to prevent the recurrence of these conflicts in the future.

This section will examine several examples of historical conflicts around the world, highlighting their origins, developments, consequences and the resolution efforts that have been undertaken. It will also show how the collective memory of these conflicts continues to influence international relations, national politics, and the way societies perceive their own history. Below are some examples of historical conflicts.

6.9.2. The Israeli-Palestinian Conflict

The Israeli-Palestinian conflict is one of the most notorious historical conflicts in multilateral meetings. Decades of tensions, wars, and deep differences between Israel and the Palestinians have made peace negotiations extremely difficult. Multilateral meetings, including under the auspices of the UN, have seen attempts to resolve the conflict, but persistent obstacles related to historical trauma and territorial claims continue to complicate the talks.

6.9.2.1. India–Pakistan Relations

The two neighbors, India and Pakistan, have relations marked by historical conflicts, particularly about the Kashmir region. Mediation attempts and multilateral meetings to resolve these disputes have been frequent, but historical disputes and political tensions remain an ongoing challenge.

6.9.2.2. Disputes in the South China Sea

Territorial claims in the South China Sea have led to historic conflicts between China, Vietnam, the Philippines, Taiwan, and other regional players. Multilateral meetings, such as discussions on the South China Sea Code of Conduct, have been used to try to resolve these complex disagreements, but territorial disputes and strategic interests continue to weigh on the negotiations.

These examples illustrate how historical conflicts can complicate multilateral meetings, making the search for common solutions and international cooperation particularly difficult. However, despite the challenges, efforts to resolve such conflicts remain essential to promote peace and stability in the world.

6.9.2.3. Geopolitical Disagreements

Geopolitical disputes can lead to diplomatic tensions, especially over issues such as borders, disputed territories, or regional allegiances. Here are some famous examples of geopolitical disagreements in multilateral meetings:

6.9.2.4. The Conflict in Ukraine

The conflict in Ukraine, particularly in Crimea and the east of the country, is an example of major geopolitical disagreement in multilateral meetings. Russia and Ukraine have antagonistic positions regarding the sovereignty of Crimea, which has led to diplomatic tensions and international sanctions. Multilateral meetings, such as the Minsk peace talks, have attempted to resolve this complex conflict.

6.9.2.5. The Conflict in Syria

The conflict in Syria has caused major geopolitical disagreements between various international actors, including Russia, the US, Iran, Turkey, and others. Divergent strategic interests, such as control of key areas and the fight against terrorism, have complicated peace negotiations and multilateral meetings aimed at ending the conflict.

These examples highlight how geopolitical disagreements, particularly those related to territorial sovereignty and strategic interests, can generate significant diplomatic tensions. Multilateral meetings are often used to try to resolve these disagreements, but they remain persistent challenges in the global diplomatic landscape.

6.9.2.6. Ideological Differences

Ideological differences are profound differences in beliefs, values and political perspectives among participants in multilateral meetings. These disagreements can make discussions complex and potentially confrontational. However, with strategic approaches, it is possible to manage these differences and foster constructive exchanges. This section explores famous examples of ideological divergences and methods for dealing with them.

6.9.2.7. The Cold War

The Cold War is one of the most emblematic examples of ideological divergences in multilateral meetings. The US and the Soviet Union were the two superpowers that opposed each other on fundamental ideological issues, including capitalism versus communism. These differences have influenced the creation of international organizations such as the UN and NATO, as well as disarmament negotiations.

6.9.2.8. Human Rights

Discussions on human rights at the UN are often the scene of ideological differences. Some countries advocate restrictive approaches to human rights, arguing that national sovereignty takes precedence, while others insist on the importance of universal human rights standards. These divergences are manifested in debates on freedom of expression, religious freedom, and other fundamental rights.

6.9.2.9. International Governance

Ideological disagreements also influence discussions on international governance. Some countries support a strong multilateral approach, while others prioritize national sovereignty and oppose foreign interference. These differences can complicate negotiations on issues such as international trade, climate change, and international security.

6.9.2.10. China–Taiwan

The ideological and political differences between mainland China and Taiwan have their roots in the complex history of relations between the two entities. Mainland China considers Taiwan a Chinese province and claims sovereignty over the island, while Taiwan considers itself a sovereign and independent State, under the official name of the Republic of China. These differences have led to persistent tensions and a lack of mutual recognition on the international stage.

Since the end of the Chinese Civil War in 1949, when the Chinese Communist Party took control of the mainland while the Nationalist government withdrew to Taiwan, the two entities have maintained tense relations. Mainland China considers

Taiwan to be an integral part of its territory and firmly opposes any form of separatism or independence of the island. It seeks to isolate Taiwan on the international stage by pushing other countries not to recognize its status as a sovereign State.

On the other hand, Taiwan has managed to develop economically and politically independently, becoming a thriving democracy with a vibrant economy and a prosperous society. However, its international status remains contested, with most countries not formally recognizing its independence.

This fragile status quo has led to diplomatic confrontations and political rivalries, particularly in multilateral forums such as the UN. Mainland China often pressures international organizations to exclude Taiwan from participation, while Taiwan seeks to maintain its presence on the world stage despite obstacles. According to one of the diplomats who answered our questions, "one of the main challenges is the diversity of opinions and interests among Member States. Each country has its own priorities and objectives, which can make discussions complex and often protracted. In addition, there are often geopolitical tensions and rivalries that can hinder the negotiation process."

Relations between mainland China and Taiwan remain one of the main sources of tension in the Asian region and continue to influence the geopolitical dynamics of the region. Efforts to peacefully resolve differences between the two sides remain a major challenge for the international community.

6.10. Solution for Managing Strained Relationships

Managing tense relations is a crucial challenge in the context of international relations and diplomacy. These tensions can arise for a variety of reasons, including political, economic, territorial, cultural, or ideological disagreements between nations. The effective management of these tense relations is essential to maintain stability, foster cooperation, and prevent conflict. This section will examine different solutions and strategies for addressing and managing these strained relationships, with a focus on diplomacy, mediation, preventive diplomacy, effective communication, compromise, and reconciliation efforts.

Diplomacy is one of the most fundamental tools for managing tense relations between nations. It involves discussions, negotiations, and talks between State representatives to resolve disagreements peacefully. Diplomatic channels are essential for keeping dialogue open, even in times of tension.

Several examples of negotiation strategies and their practical applications are summarized in Table 6.

Table 6: Illustrating Strategies for Multilateral Diplomatic Negotiations

Trading Strategy	Description	When to Use It	Examples in Practice
Win-win strategy	Both sides leave the negotiating table with gains	Multilateral treaties, trade agreements	Paris Climate Agreement
Compromise	Both sides make concessions to reach an agreement	Conflict resolution	Peace agreements in conflict zones
Difficult negotiation	One side takes a firm stance and aims to get as many concessions as possible	High-stakes negotiations	Negotiations on nuclear disarmament
Collaborative problem-solving	Parties work together to find mutually beneficial solutions	Complex issues requiring cooperation	Managing global health crises, such as COVID-19 responses

This table offers a summary of presentation techniques with descriptions and examples to facilitate their understanding and application. You can adjust or enrich these few techniques according to your specificities or requirements.

Mediation is another important approach. Neutral third parties, such as international organizations or friendly countries, can play a mediating role to facilitate discussions between the parties to the conflict and help them reach agreements. Mediation can help to defuse tensions and create space for negotiated solutions.

Preventive diplomacy aims to anticipate and defuse potential conflicts before they escalate. It usually involves dialogue, confidence-building, and mediation measures in areas where tensions already exist, but where large-scale conflict could be avoided with appropriate intervention.

Effective communication is a key part of managing strained relationships. Diplomats and leaders must ensure that they maintain open, transparent, and constructive communication with their foreign counterparts. Poorly managed communication can escalate tensions, while constructive communication can help find common solutions.

Compromises also play a central role. Often, strained relationships can be eased by finding solutions that consider the concerns and interests of both parties. Mutual give-and-take can help create common ground and reduce tensions.

Finally, reconciliation efforts are essential to resolve past conflicts and heal strained relations. Reconciliation can include symbolic gestures, a formal apology, truth and reconciliation processes, and reparations for victims.

This section will explore these different solutions in detail, using historical and contemporary examples to illustrate how they have been successfully implemented in the past and how they can be applied to manage strained relationships in the future.

6.10.1. Persevering Dialogue

Open and persistent dialogue is essential. Diplomats must maintain channels of communication to try to resolve disagreements. Persistent dialogue is an essential component of diplomacy and the resolution of international conflicts. It refers to the willingness to maintain discussions and negotiations even when tensions are high and obstacles seem insurmountable. This approach is based on the belief that, even in the most difficult situations, peaceful solutions can be achieved through perseverance, patience, and commitment to dialogue.

When international relations are tense, it is often tempting to break off dialogue or withdraw from negotiations due to frustration, anger, or impatience. However, persevering dialogue involves resisting this temptation and maintaining an open channel of communication, even when talks seem to be stagnating or the parties are in deep disagreement.

Persistent dialogue can be particularly important in protracted and intractable conflicts, such as territorial, ethnic, or religious conflicts. In such situations, it may be necessary to continue discussions for many years or even decades before a lasting agreement is reached. A notable example is the peace process in Northern Ireland, which lasted for years before culminating in the Good Friday Agreement in 1998. Key elements of persevering dialogue include:

1. *Willingness to Continue*: The parties involved must be committed to maintaining dialogue, even in the face of setbacks or difficult times.
2. *Patience*: Negotiations can be long and complex. Patience is key to resolving difficult issues.
3. *Commitment to Peaceful Resolution*: All parties must believe in the possibility of a peaceful solution and be determined to avoid violence.

4. *Inclusion*: Persistent dialogue may require the inclusion of diverse actors, including marginalized groups or local stakeholders.
5. *Mediation and Facilitation*: Sometimes neutral third parties or mediators are needed to help maintain dialogue and find solutions.
6. *Flexibility*: The parties must be willing to adapt their positions and make compromises to move forward.

The example of persevering dialogue in the international context can be illustrated by the Middle East peace talks, which have lasted for decades without reaching a final solution. Despite many obstacles, negotiators and mediators have persisted in their efforts to find a peaceful solution to the Israeli-Palestinian conflict.

Persistent dialogue is a powerful tool for resolving international conflicts and maintaining global stability. He recalled that, even in the darkest moments, diplomacy and dialogue have the potential to turn tense relations into opportunities for peace and cooperation.

6.10.2. Focus on Common Interests

Rather than focusing on differences, delegations can seek common interests and shared goals. Finding pragmatic solutions can help ease tensions. Focusing on common interests is a fundamental approach to diplomacy and international negotiations aimed at resolving conflicts and promoting cooperation between nations. This strategy is based on the idea that, even in situations of deep disagreement, there are often areas of shared interest that can serve as a basis for mutually beneficial agreements and solutions.

When international relations are tense or conflictual, the parties involved often have divergent concerns, priorities, and objectives. However, by identifying and emphasizing common interests, it is possible to create common ground where parties can work together to achieve shared goals. This approach is based on the principles of preventive diplomacy and peaceful conflict resolution. Key elements of focusing on common interests include:

1. *Identification of Shared Interests*: Negotiators must first understand the priorities and concerns of all parties involved in the conflict. This requires a careful analysis of the positions and motivations of each side.
2. *Finding Points of Convergence*: Once common interests have been identified, negotiators can work to find areas where the parties' objectives

align. These can be humanitarian issues, regional security, the economy, the environment, etc.

3. *Building Trust*: Focusing on common interests can help build trust between parties. Successful cooperation in one area can pave the way for a comprehensive resolution of the conflict.
4. *Preventive Diplomacy*: By anticipating potential conflicts and working to resolve problems before they escalate, nations can avoid major crises.
5. *Finding Mutually Beneficial Solutions*: Agreements made by focusing on common interests are more likely to be sustainable, as they provide benefits to all parties. This can help with the implementation and enforcement of agreements.

A concrete example of the focus on common interests is the 1959 Antarctic Treaty, which established the Antarctic continent as an area of peaceful scientific research. The treaty signatories had diverse interests, but they managed to put aside their differences to focus on scientific exploration and environmental preservation of Antarctica, creating a space for sustainable international cooperation.

In conclusion, focusing on common interests is an effective diplomatic strategy for resolving international conflicts and promoting cooperation among nations. It is based on understanding shared priorities and finding mutually beneficial solutions, thereby contributing to stability and global peace.

6.10.3. External Mediation

Sometimes, the involvement of a third party, such as a neutral mediator or an international organization, may be necessary to facilitate the talks. For example, negotiations over Iran's nuclear program have been the scene of strained diplomatic relations between Iran and several Western countries, particularly the US. Despite these tensions, the talks culminated in the Vienna Agreement in 2015, demonstrating the possibility of cooperation in difficult situations.[2]

So, managing strained diplomatic relations requires subtle diplomacy, a willingness to set aside historical disagreements, and the ability to find mutually beneficial solutions. In a multilateral context, cooperation in the face of friction can help to solve complex global problems and promote peace and stability.

---

[2] This document is available in open access via the following link: https://www.diplomatie.gouv.fr/IMG/pdf/2015_07_14_-_factsheet_-_accord_sur_le_nucleaire_iranien_cle4cd9a4.pdf

6.10.4. Maintaining Mutual Respect

Mutual respect remains a fundamental principle in multilateral meetings. Delegations should strive to maintain a respectful and constructive tone, even if there were deep disagreements among participants. Mutual respect creates a climate for open exchange and encourages the possibility of building bridges of understanding.

6.10.5. Commitment to the Multilateral Process

Bilateral tensions should not impede engagement in the multilateral process. Multilateral meetings are opportunities for countries to collaborate and find common solutions to global challenges. Even when relations are strained, it is crucial to maintain active participation in discussions and contribute to consensus-building.

As such, commitment to the multilateral process is a key element of diplomacy and international relations. It refers to the willingness of a State or organization to actively participate in forums, treaties, agreements, and other mechanisms of international cooperation involving several parties. This commitment is essential to promote peace, security, sustainable development, and the resolution of global problems. Commitment to the multilateral process is manifested in several ways, including:

1. *Active Participation*: States and organizations actively participate in the negotiations, discussions, and activities of multilateral organizations such as the UN, the World Trade Organization (WTO), and the World Health Organization (WHO). They contribute by providing their expertise, their resources and by respecting the commitments made.
2. *Respect for International Law*: Multilateral actors commit to respect the principles of international law, including respect for treaties and agreements to which they have acceded. This strengthens credibility and confidence in the multilateral system.
3. *Promotion of Common Values*: Commitment to the multilateral process involves the promotion of common international values and standards such as human rights, democracy, the rule of law, and social justice.
4. *Peaceful Conflict Resolution*: Multilateral actors commit to resolving international conflicts through peaceful means, such as mediation, preventive diplomacy, and dispute resolution mechanisms.

5. *Economic Cooperation and Sustainable Development*: Commitment to
    the multilateral process involves cooperation in areas such as international
    trade, development assistance, poverty alleviation, environmental protec-
    tion, and the management of global resources.

Engagement in the multilateral process is essential to address complex global
challenges such as climate change, food security, pandemics, terrorism, migration, and many others. It enables nations to work together to find effective and
equitable solutions that benefit the entire international community.

A notable example of the commitment to the multilateral process is the 2015
Paris Climate Agreement (Bettati 2012). This agreement has been signed by
196 countries,[3] showing a collective commitment to fight climate change. Each
country has developed its own Nationally Determined Contributions, but the
common goal is to limit global warming to below 2°C.

In conclusion, commitment to the multilateral process is a fundamental pillar
of international diplomacy. It promotes peace, cooperation, and the resolution of
global problems, and it is essential to meet the challenges of the twenty-first century.

6.10.6. Quiet Diplomacy

In situations where relations between certain countries are particularly tense, it
can be useful to resort to discreet diplomacy in advance of multilateral meetings.
Unofficial communication channels can be used to address specific concerns and
friction points. This approach allows countries to clarify their positions, reduce
misunderstandings and create a more favorable ground for formal negotiations.

Quiet diplomacy, often referred to as "silent diplomacy" or "behind-the-scenes
diplomacy," is an approach to diplomacy characterized by negotiations and diplomatic
activities conducted in a confidential manner, away from the media spotlight and the
public. This form of diplomacy takes place mostly in private, and the results of talks
are usually not revealed until an agreement is reached, or significant progress has
been made. Quiet diplomacy has several key characteristics and benefits, including:

1. *Confidentiality*: Confidential diplomatic discussions allow the parties to
    speak more openly and discuss sensitive issues without the pressure of
    public opinion. This promotes a more honest and open dialogue.

[3.] This document is available online: https://unfccc.int/files/meetings/paris_nov_2015/application/pdf/paris_
agreement_french_.pdf.

2. *Flexibility*: Negotiators can explore different options and trade-offs without the constraint of fixed public positions. This can make it easier to find creative solutions to complex problems.

3. *Crisis Management*: Quiet diplomacy is often used to de-escalate conflicts, resolve crises, and prevent escalations. It allows the parties to the conflict to work behind the scenes to find solutions before the situation escalates.

4. *Public Relations Protection*: When talks fail or are difficult, quiet diplomacy helps avoid[4] embarrassing public failures and preserves the public relations of the parties involved.

5. *Face Preservation*: Governments may be more willing to make concessions or compromise when they can do so without losing face to their public opinion or electoral base.

6. *Managing Sensitive International Issues*: Quiet diplomacy is often used to deal with sensitive international issues such as nuclear proliferation, counterterrorism, peace agreements, and treaty negotiations.

7. *Reducing Tensions*: By avoiding making certain discussions public, quiet diplomacy can help reduce tensions and create a climate conducive to more formal talks.

It is important to note that quiet diplomacy is not without its controversies. Some critics see it as lacking transparency and accountability, as it often escapes public and media scrutiny. However, its proponents argue that its effectiveness in resolving conflicts and negotiating complex agreements makes it an essential diplomatic tool.

A recent example of quiet diplomacy is the role played by international mediators in the peace negotiations in Afghanistan in 2020. These negotiations, aimed at ending decades of conflict, were preceded by confidential discussions between the parties to the conflict and international mediators. These behind-the-scenes discussions eventually led to the opening of formal talks.

In summary, quiet diplomacy is an essential approach to international diplomacy, allowing parties to negotiate confidentially and seek pragmatic solutions to complex problems. It is particularly useful for resolving conflicts, managing crises, and dealing with sensitive international issues.

---

4. *Case of Diplomatic Failure Due to Mismanaged Communication*: In 1999, the clumsiness of a speech by British Prime Minister Tony Blair on Kosovo led to tensions with his NATO allies.

6.10.7. Finding Common Solutions

The goal of multilateral meetings is to reach common solutions to global challenges. Countries need to put aside their bilateral differences and focus on collective interests and shared goals. By working together to address global challenges such as climate change, poverty or security, bilateral tensions can temporarily recede, thus allowing a neutral ground for cooperation.

The search for common solutions, also known as the search for shared solutions or mutually beneficial solutions, is a fundamental approach in diplomacy and conflict resolution at the international level. It is about finding answers to problems that not only satisfy the interests and concerns of the parties in conflict but are also acceptable and beneficial to all parties involved. This approach is based on several key principles:

1. *Collaboration*: The search for common solutions relies on cooperation between the parties involved. Rather than confronting each other in an intransigent confrontation, the parties work together to identify points of agreement and work out compromises.
2. *Open Communication*: Open communication and transparency are key to understanding the concerns, needs and interests of all parties. This creates an environment conducive to finding mutually beneficial solutions.
3. *Fairness*: The solutions sought must be fair, ensuring that each party receives an equal benefit and that no one is unfairly disadvantaged.
4. *Creativity*: Finding common solutions encourages creativity and innovative thinking to overcome obstacles and reach satisfactory compromises.
5. *Pragmatism*: It is based on the achievement of realistic and achievable objectives. Joint solutions are rooted in feasibility and efficiency.
6. *Win-Win*: The goal is to achieve a win-win situation, where all parties benefit from the agreement reached. This may require concessions on both sides, but the emphasis is on mutual benefits.

The search for common solutions is commonly used in diplomacy to resolve international conflicts, negotiate trade and environmental agreements, and address other complex issues. It is also a pillar of multilateral negotiations, where many parties are involved and where finding common ground is essential.

A concrete example of the search for common solutions is the 2015 Paris Climate Agreement. As part of this agreement, countries around the world have worked together to develop a set of greenhouse gas emission reduction targets. The agreement was designed in such a way that each country can set its own targets according to its national capacities and priorities, while collectively contributing to the common goal of combating climate change.

In summary, the search for common solutions is a crucial approach to resolving conflicts and negotiating international agreements. It is based on collaboration, open communication, fairness, creativity, and pragmatism, with the aim of achieving mutually beneficial results for all parties involved.

6.10.8. Strengthening Ties Through Common Interests

Multilateral meetings also provide an opportunity to strengthen ties between countries through common interests. By identifying potential areas of cooperation and working together on concrete projects, countries can gradually ease tensions and build a solid foundation for more stable and positive relations.

Ultimately, managing strained diplomatic relations in multilateral encounters requires a combination of respect, constructive engagement, and skillful diplomacy. While bilateral disagreements may persist, a focus on global cooperation and the search for common solutions can help create an environment conducive to the peaceful resolution of conflicts and the promotion of global well-being.

6.10.9. Transparency and Confidentiality

Transparency and confidentiality are sensitive issues in multilateral meetings. It is important to follow established rules and procedures for information disclosure and confidentiality when necessary. Maintaining a balance between transparency and confidentiality is essential to promote trust and credibility in the multilateral process.

By proactively addressing these challenges and using the proposed solutions, you will be able to effectively navigate multilateral meetings and contribute positively to international diplomacy.

In conclusion, multilateral meetings present unique challenges, such as language and cultural barriers, complex issues, differences of opinion, lack of time and resources, strained diplomatic relations, and issues of transparency and confidentiality. By developing communication, collaboration, and problem-solving skills, you will be able to address these challenges and foster constructive and mutually beneficial outcomes in multilateral meetings.

CHAPTER 7

The Functioning of the United Nations General Assembly

Multilateral meetings take a variety of forms depending on their objectives, the structure of the participants, and the areas of interest. The UN General Assembly is the largest platform for discussion that brings together all the countries of the world. Established in 1945 under the Charter of the UN, the General Assembly occupies a central position as the principal body for discussion, policy formulation, and representation of the UN. It is composed of the 193 Member States of the UN and provides a unique forum for multilateral dialogues on all international issues set out in the Charter. In addition, it plays a central role in setting norms and creating international laws (Nations Unies 2023).

7.1. Functions and Powers of the General Assembly

The UN General Assembly plays a major role in developing recommendations to Member States on various international issues within its competence. It has also acted in a multitude of areas within the UN, including political, economic, humanitarian, social, and legal aspects. The Assembly meets annually from September to December for its main session, and from January to September, as required, including to consider the reports of the Fourth and Fifth Committees. During the resumed session, the Assembly considers contemporary issues of critical importance to the international community through high-level thematic debates organized by the presidency of the General Assembly, in consultation with Member States. During this period, the Assembly also holds traditional informal consultations on a wide range of key issues with a view to the adoption of new resolutions.

In September 2015, the General Assembly marked a significant milestone by adopting the seventeen Sustainable Development Goals enshrined in the outcome document of the UN Summit on the adoption of the post-2015 development

An Image of the President of the 79th United Nations
General Assembly Presiding over a Plenary Session

agenda, known as resolution A/RES/70/1, entitled *Transforming Our World: The 2030 Agenda for Sustainable Development*. These ambitious goals aim to address critical global issues.

In 2022, the General Assembly convened a series of meetings to review and discuss the recommendations presented by the Secretary-General in his report entitled *Our Common Agenda*. The Programme of Action is designed to strengthen and accelerate the implementation of multilateral agreements, with a particular focus on the 2030 Agenda for Sustainable Development. The goal is to concretely improve the living conditions of people around the world.

Under the Charter of the UN, the functions of the General Assembly are:

- To review and approve the budget of the UN and to determine the level of assessments of Member States;
- To elect the non-permanent members of the Security Council and members of other councils and organs of the UN and, on the recommendation of the Security Council, to appoint the Secretary-General;
- To study and make recommendations on the general principles of cooperation in the maintenance of international peace and security, including disarmament;
- Discuss and, except when a dispute or situation is under consideration by the Security Council, make recommendations on any matter relating to international peace and security;

- To discuss, with the same exception, all matters within the scope of the Charter or relating to the powers and functions of any organ of the UN, and to make recommendations thereon;
- To initiate studies and make recommendations with a view to developing international cooperation in the political field, encouraging the development and codification of international law, facilitating the enjoyment of human rights and fundamental freedoms, and international cooperation in the economic, social, humanitarian, cultural, educational, and health fields;
- To make recommendations to enable the peaceful settlement of any situation that could jeopardize friendly relations between countries; and
- To study reports of the Security Council and other UN bodies.

It should be noted that the Assembly may also act in the event of a threat to the peace, a breach of the peace, or an act of aggression, if the Security Council has been unable to act because of the negative vote of a permanent member. In such cases, in accordance with its resolution entitled *Uniting for Peace* of November 3, 1950,[1] the Assembly may immediately consider the matter and recommend to its members the adoption of collective measures to maintain or restore international peace and security.

7.1.1. Procedures and Rules for Debate in the United Nations General Assembly

In multilateral meetings in international organizations such as the UN, the speaking time given to each speaker plays a crucial role in managing debates and facilitating constructive discussions. The UN General Assembly, under its Rules of Procedure, implements rigorous procedures to ensure constructive, balanced, and orderly debates. Indeed, it is rules 68 to 81 of the rules of procedure (A/520/Rev.20) that establish a detailed framework for the management of speaking time, points of order, rights of reply, and other crucial aspects of discussions in the Assembly. We review the articles in question in the lines below.

7.1.1.1. Article 68: Authorization to Speak and Scheduling

This article establishes a fundamental basis for the management of interventions at the UN General Assembly. It stipulates that no one may speak without first

---

[1] Online: https://documents-dds-ny.un.org/doc/RESOLUTION/GEN/NR0/060/97/PDF/NR006097.pdf?OpenElement.

obtaining the authorization of the President. This provision is essential to ensure an orderly conduct of the proceedings by avoiding unplanned interruptions. Moreover, the fact that the Chairperson gives the floor to speakers in the order in which they have requested it promotes fairness and prevents any bias in the selection of speakers. The possibility for the President to call to order a speaker whose remarks are off-topic also enhances the quality of the discussions by maintaining the focus on the issues on the agenda.

7.1.1.2. Article 69: Priority Round for Commissions

This article highlights the special consideration given to Committee Chairs and Rapporteurs. The granting of a priority round allows the leaders of these bodies to effectively present the conclusions of their work. This not only informs the General Assembly about the performance of the commissions but also enhances the role of these bodies in the overall decision-making process.

7.1.1.3. Rule 70: Statements by the Secretariat

This article recognizes the relevance of the contributions of the Secretary-General and his representatives to the debates. The authorization of the Secretary-General or a designated member of the Secretariat to make oral or written statements on any matter under consideration by the Assembly strengthens the advisory and informative role of the Secretariat. This provision allows members of the Assembly to benefit from additional expertise and analysis to inform their deliberations.

7.1.1.4. Rule 71: Points of Order

This article establishes a mechanism to maintain order and coherence in discussions. Points of order allow a representative to raise a concern about the process or content of the debate that is taking place. The fact that the Speaker rules immediately on these motions helps to keep the debate flowing. The ability of any representative to challenge the Speaker's ruling on appeal and to put the matter to a vote enhances transparency and fairness in the handling of these motions.

7.1.1.5. Article 72: Limitation of Speaking Time

This article reflects the concern to manage speaking time effectively to promote balanced and efficient discussions. The possibility for the Assembly to limit the speaking time of each speaker and each representative on the same issue recognizes the importance of giving the floor to as many participants as possible while avoiding excessively long speeches. The requirement to hear speakers for and against a proposal to set such limits demonstrates a concern for inclusiveness and diversity of opinion.

7.1.1.6. Rule 73: Closure of the List of Speakers and Right of Reply

This article balances the closure of speakers' lists with the possibility of responding to speeches delivered after the closure. This flexibility allows the President to adequately manage debates while responding to unexpected developments. The right of reply given to a member when post-closing speeches make it timely ensures that discussions remain dynamic and adaptable to circumstances.[2]

7.1.1.7. Rule 74: Debate Adjourned

This rule sets out a formal process for requesting the adjournment of a debate. Putting adjournment motions to a vote after interventions for and against ensures transparent decision-making. The possibility for the Speaker to limit the length of speeches under this Standing Order is intended to maintain temporal discipline while allowing for substantive debate.

7.1.1.8. Rule 75: Closure of the Debate

This rule gives representatives the possibility of requesting the closure of a debate. The procedure for putting the motion to a vote after speeches for and against ensures that different perspectives are considered. The Speaker's discretion to limit the length of interventions under this Standing Order maintains the effectiveness of the proceedings.

[2.] *The Right of Reply to the United Nations*: During debates at the UN, a State can exercise its right of reply if a statement made by another country is perceived as erroneous or offensive. This mechanism is often used in conflicts between Israel and Arab countries.

7.1.1.9. Rule 76: Suspension or Adjournment of the Sitting

This rule provides a mechanism for suspending or adjourning the sitting. Putting motions to this effect immediately ensures that these decisions are made quickly, thus avoiding prolonged disruption. The possibility for the President to limit the duration of the intervention of the representative proposing the suspension or adjournment maintains temporal consistency.

7.1.1.10. Rule 77: Order of Procedural Motions

This rule sets out the order of precedence of procedural motions, laying the groundwork for organizing discussions in an orderly manner. By prioritizing motions to suspend, adjourn, adjourn, and close debate, the rule establishes a hierarchy of procedures to maintain the structure and effectiveness of discussions.

7.1.1.11. Article 78: Proposals and Amendments

This article highlights the importance of the preparation and prior distribution of proposals and amendments. The rule that proposals must be circulated to all delegations prior to the meeting ensures that members have the necessary time to review and prepare to discuss these elements. The possibility for the President to allow the discussion of amendments and procedural motions that have not been circulated enhances the flexibility of the process.

7.1.1.12. Article 79: Decisions on Jurisdiction

This rule sets out a logical sequence for debate by requiring that motions on jurisdiction be put to a vote before the vote on the proposal. This ensures that the issue of competence is dealt with before the Assembly takes a final decision on the content of the proposal.

7.1.1.13. Rule 80: Withdrawal of Motions

This rule allows authors to withdraw their motions before they are put to the vote, if they have not been amended. This rule provides flexibility for representatives to adjust their positions and contributions during the debate.

7.1.1.14. Article 81: Reconsideration of Proposals

This article establishes a rule limiting the reconsideration of proposals adopted or rejected. The provision requires a qualified majority to reconsider a proposal already decided during the same session, stressing the importance of decision-making stability while allowing for revisions in cases of pressing need.

These articles set out the essential rules that guide discussions at the UN General Assembly, ensuring that debates are organized, fair, and lead to informed decisions. By combining these rules, the rules of procedure of the General Assembly create a structured and balanced framework for the conduct of multilateral debates within the UN. These rules promote equitable participation, effective discussions, and informed decision-making.

7.2. The General Debate of the General Assembly

The annual general debate of the UN General Assembly is of considerable importance as a global forum where Member States can express their views on major international issues. It is a major event in international diplomacy, bringing together leaders from around the world to discuss global challenges.[3]

During this debate, which takes place every September, heads of State and Government, as well as foreign ministers, take the floor to share their perspectives on issues such as international peace and security, sustainable development, human rights, climate change, regional conflicts, and many more. Each Member State has a time slot to present its speech, which can address national concerns, regional priorities, or global issues.

[3.] Tentative timeline
- *Opening of the 78th session of the General Assembly*: September 5, 2023.
- *For your information, here is the list of themes that are discussed during the high-level meetings held in the framework of the 78th UNGA*:
- High-Level Political Forum on Sustainable Development: September 18–19, 2023—Organized under the auspices of the General Assembly.
- *General Debate*: Tuesday, September 19, to Saturday, September 23, and Tuesday, September 26, 2023—Website coming soon.
- *High-Level Dialogue on Financing for Development*: September 20, 2023—Resolution A/RES/69/313.
- *High-Level Meeting on Pandemic Prevention, Preparedness and Response*: September 20, 2023—Resolution A/RES/77/275.
- Climate Ambition Summit: September 20, 2023—Organized by the Secretary-General.
- *High-Level Meeting on Universal Health Coverage*: September 21, 2023—Resolution A/RES/75/315.
- *Ministerial Preparatory Meeting for the Summit of the Future*: September 21, 2023—Resolution A/RES/76/307.
- *High-Level Meeting on TB Control*: September 22, 2023—Resolution A/RES/77/274.
- *High-Level Plenary Meeting to Celebrate and Promote the* International Day for the Total Elimination of Nuclear Weapons: September 26, 2023—Resolution A/RES/77/47.

A View of the General Assembly During the
General Debate on the 79th Session

A particularly significant moment during the general debate is the presentation of the report of the Secretary-General of the UN on the work of the Organization. The report is usually presented by the Secretary-General on the opening day of the debate. It offers an overview of the UN's activities and initiatives over the past year, as well as the challenges and opportunities ahead. The Secretary-General's report is a key document that guides discussions and decisions in the General Assembly.

The annual general debate of the General Assembly is an essential platform for international dialogue, preventive diplomacy, and consensus-building. It allows Member States to promote their positions, seek partnerships, mobilize international support, and advance global initiatives. It is also a time for world leaders to engage directly and discuss solutions to the most pressing problems facing the international community. Ultimately, the general debate reinforces the central role of the UN as a multilateral forum for cooperation and the resolution of global problems.

7.3. Debate in the Main Committees[4]

Following the general debate, the UN General Assembly begins its consideration of the substantive issues on its agenda.[5] In view of the large number of items to be addressed, the Assembly divides these issues among six Main Committees, "each of which is responsible for a specific area of competence. These Main Committees consider issues related to the agenda items and make recommendations in the form of draft resolutions and decisions for further consideration and action by the General Assembly.

The six Main Committees are organized according to their areas of expertise, which allows for an effective division of responsibilities and a more specialized approach to each issue. Each Main Committee is composed of representatives of UN member states and is chaired by an elected member of the General Assembly.

These commissions address a wide range of topics, including political, economic, financial, social, humanitarian, cultural and educational, disarmament, and international security issues. They review proposals, discuss the views of Member States and work to develop texts of resolutions and decisions that will serve as a basis for future UN action in these areas.

Once draft resolutions and decisions are prepared in the Main Committees, they are submitted to the General Assembly as part of its agenda. Member states debate and vote on these tests to determine the actions to be taken, the policies to be adopted and the measures to be implemented within the UN. The work of the Main Committees plays a critical role in formulating international policies and actions undertaken by the UN to respond to global challenges.

Several agenda items, including the question of Palestine and the situation in the Middle East, are considered directly in the plenary meeting of the General Assembly.

[4.] *The six Main Committees are*:
  1. the Committee on Disarmament and International Security (First Committee);
  2. the Economic and Financial Committee (Second Committee);
  3. the Committee on Social, Humanitarian and Cultural Issues (Third Committee);
  4. the Special Political and Decolonization Committee (Fourth Committee);
  5. the Committee on Administrative and Budgetary Questions (Fifth Committee); and
  6. the Committee on Legal Affairs (Sixth Committee).

[5.] See, for example, the agenda (A/78/150) of the 78th UNGA Opening at United Nations Headquarters, in New York, on Tuesday, September 5, 2023, at 3 p.m.: https://documents-dds-ny.un.org/doc/UNDOC/GEN/N23/182/49/PDF/N2318249.pdf?OpenElement.

7.4. Plenary Meetings of the General Assembly and Meetings of the Bureau

The UN General Assembly, as the organization's main deliberative body, plays a critical role in decision-making on critical global issues. The plenary meetings of the Assembly and the meetings of the Bureau are of great importance for discussions, negotiations, and the definition of future directions. In the following lines, we provide an overview of the timing and revitalization of these sessions:

7.4.1. Calendar of Plenary Sessions

The calendar of plenary meetings of the General Assembly is a vital element in coordinating the work, debates, and decisions. However, for the current session (January 1, 2023–September 2023), there is no pre-established work program for the meetings, whether formal or informal. The draft program of work for the plenary meetings for the session was presented in the report of the Secretary-General on the revitalization of the work of the General Assembly (A/76/903).[6]

Table of Meetings Scheduled in the Various United Nations Rooms

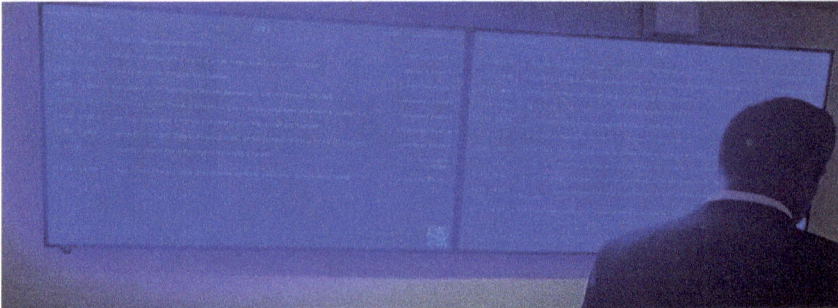

[6.] "The present report has been prepared pursuant to paragraph 5 (d) of the annex to General Assembly resolution 58/316. It contains the draft program of work for the plenary meetings of the Assembly at its seventy-seventh session. The draft program of work may be revised further, in the light of decisions that the Assembly may have to take due to the situation created by the coronavirus disease 2019 (COVID-19). The draft programs of work of five of the six Main Committees of the Assembly, which have been adopted by the Assembly, are contained in the respective decisions of the Assembly; they could also be reviewed in the light of decisions that the Main Committees or the Assembly might have to take because of the situation created by COVID-19. The status of the documentation will be included in an addendum to this report," see the full text via the following link: https://documents-dds-ny.un.org/doc/UNDOC/GEN/N22/428/42/PDF/N2242842.pdf?OpenElement.

This report aims to improve the effectiveness and relevance of the discussions and decisions taken during the plenary sessions.

7.4.2. Revitalization of the Work of the General Assembly

The revitalization of the work of the General Assembly is an initiative to strengthen, and its aim is to make the debates more focused, to enable faster decision-making and to increase the impact of the resolutions adopted.

7.4.3. Announcements in the Journal of the United Nations[7]

To ensure the transparency and accessibility of plenary meetings, the dates and times of the meetings will be announced in the *Journal of the United Nations* once they have been scheduled. This approach allows delegations and observers to plan their participation and follow the discussions promptly.

In summary, the plenary meetings of the General Assembly and the meetings of the Bureau are crucial moments when representatives of member states come together to discuss, negotiate, and take decisions that will have a global impact. The timing and revitalization of the work contribute to making these sessions more effective and relevant spaces to address global issues and shape the future of international cooperation.

7.4.4. e-deleGATE Portal[8] and Plenary Place

The Department for General Assembly and Conference Management has centralized the digital services available to members of delegations on the e-deleGATE portal (https://edelegate.un.int/). This password-protected portal is an essential resource for delegates attending multilateral meetings within the UN.

It is an online platform used by delegates to access various information and documents related to meetings. It provides a centralized space where delegates can view the agenda, working papers, proposed resolutions, and relevant reports.

[7.] Link to the Journal: https://journal.un.org/fr/new-york/all/2023-09-05.

[8.] https://edelegate.un.int/.

The portal also allows delegates to submit amendments, participate in debates and vote, electronically.

Therefore, this portal facilitates communication between delegates by providing features such as discussion forums, mailing lists, and automatic notifications. It also allows you to manage meeting registrations, view delegate profiles, and schedule bilateral or informal meetings.

Among others, this portal contains important elements such as: **General information** that provides convenient access to essential general information, such as official documents, the *Journal of the United Nations*, and UN News. These resources are crucial to staying informed of current developments within the UN. Then there are **the online services that allow** members of delegations to use various online services through the portal, including **e-registration**, which promotes the online registration of members of delegations participating in meetings.

Then, the **e-Speakers** module allows the registration on the list of speakers for the planned interventions. **The system** is an electronic platform specifically designed for the registration of speakers for plenary meetings of the General Assembly. This digital platform[9] makes it easy to manage speaker lists, allowing for efficient planning and organization of sessions. At the level of Permanent Missions, this function is often entrusted to a person designated as the focal point.

Also, there is the **e-Proposals** function, which allows the submission of draft resolutions to the General Assembly, its Main Committees, and its subsidiary bodies. Finally, there is a **plenary space** that is reserved for the communication of letters addressed by the President of the General Assembly to the permanent representatives and observers to the UN in New York.

It is important to note that the Plenary Space, also known as the Plenary Place, is a virtual meeting room where the plenary sessions of multilateral meetings take place. It provides an interactive environment where delegates can participate in debates, speak, ask questions, and express their positions.

The plenary space is equipped with an advanced video conferencing system that allows delegates to connect from different locations around the world. Delegates can intervene live via their camera and microphone or through written messages.

---

[9] Today, world leaders are using Twitter to quickly disseminate their diplomatic positions, as illustrated by Donald Trump's diplomacy.

Simultaneous translation features are also available to facilitate communication between delegates speaking different languages.

In addition to the live debates, the Plenary Space also allows for the broadcasting of presentations, videos, and other relevant content. It also offers time management tools to respect the time limits allocated to each delegate and ensure a smooth flow of plenary sessions.

A diplomat said:

> Time management is key when preparing and delivering speeches. We establish a clear timetable for the drafting, revision, and finalization of the speech, considering the deadlines imposed by the agenda of the General Assembly or the Security Council. We are working closely with our team to meet these deadlines and ensure that the speech is ready in time for its presentation.

These technological tools, such as the e-deleGATE portal and the Plenary Space, are essential to facilitate exchanges and decision-making processes at multilateral meetings. They enable delegates to actively participate, collaborate effectively, and engage in constructive discussions, thus contributing to the achievement of the goals of the UN.

View of an Intervention by the Permanent Representative of Haiti to the United Nations at a Security Council Meeting on Haiti on October 22, 2024

7.4.5. Access Management

Access to the e-deleGATE portal is managed by administrators within each Permanent Mission. It is these administrators who assign their mission representatives permissions to access specific parts of the portal. In addition, they can create new accesses via the management module. New representatives are encouraged to contact their mission administrator to obtain access to the portal and receive the necessary authorizations to use online services. If you have any questions or need assistance, administrators can email *missions-support@un.int.*

7.4.6. Submission of Declarations

From all the above, we can deduce that the **e-deleGATE** portal plays a critical role in the digital management of multilateral meetings at the UN, providing delegates with seamless access to the information, online services, and functionalities needed to participate in discussions and deliberations actively and effectively within the international organization. By following these procedures, delegations contribute to the efficient conduct of multilateral meetings at the UN and to the transparent availability of statements to all participants and the public.

It should be noted that questions concerning individual committees should be sent to the secretariat of the committee concerned, while questions concerning the plenary, and the portal should be addressed to the General Assembly Affairs Branch (gaab@un.org). The e-deleGATE portal and the Plenary Place are two technological tools used at multilateral meetings at the UN to facilitate procedures and improve the efficiency of delegates.

7.4.7. Registration of Speakers and Use of the e-Speakers System

The registration of speakers and the effective management of the list of speakers are crucial elements in ensuring the smooth running of the plenary meetings of the UN General Assembly. Member States' Permanent Missions play a key role in this process, using the e-Speakers system through the e-deleGATE portal to register speakers and facilitate coordination. Liaison officers are responsible for registering speakers using the e-Speakers system. They provide relevant information such as the name of the speaker, the title of the delegation, the topic of the speech, and other necessary details such as the agenda item on which the speaker wishes to speak. Delegations need to respect the procedures for submitting statements at multilateral meetings at the UN. Here is a summary of the important steps to follow.

7.4.7.1. Required Format[10]

Delegations should prepare the text of their statements in the following formats, if possible: PDF and Microsoft Word. This ensures compatibility with UN document management systems.

7.4.7.2. Sending by email

Delegations are required to send their statements by email to the eStatements section of the *Journal* (estatements@un.org). It is crucial to respect this communication channel for the submission of declarations. Delegations are often asked to send their statements by email well in advance of the scheduled meeting, at least two hours before the meeting. Once sent, an automatic acknowledgment is sent to the sender of the message. This allows the competent services to process the declaration and make it available online.

Subject of the email: In the subject line of the email and the header of the statement, it is necessary to indicate the following information: the title of the session, the name of the speaker, and the agenda item corresponding to the statement.

Online: Only statements that have been delivered during a meeting will be posted online in the eStatements section of the *Journal*. It is, therefore, crucial to meet the submission deadlines to ensure the online availability of the declaration.

Assistance and Questions: If there are any problems with the registration of speakers, Permanent Missions can request assistance. Email addresses gaspeakerslist@un.org and galindo@un.org are provided for assistance when needed. This ensures that missions have access to direct support to resolve any technical or logistical issues. If you have any questions or concerns regarding eStatements, delegations may contact the Chief of the Meetings Support Section at chiefmssdgacm@un.org.

---

[10] It should be noted that the submitted statements will not be posted online until they have been delivered at the corresponding session.

7.4.8. Cooperation and Coordination

Cooperation and coordination among Permanent Missions are essential to avoid duplication, ensure equitable distribution of speaking time, and maintain the agenda. The use of the e-Speakers system facilitates this coordination by centralizing speaker information.

7.4.9. Ensuring Readiness

Pre-registration of speakers ensures adequate preparation for plenary sessions. This gives organizers an overview of the speakers and their topics, making it easier to manage discussions and follow up on decisions.

In summary, the use of the e-Speakers system and collaboration among Permanent Missions are key elements in managing the list of speakers at the plenary meetings of the General Assembly. This ensures the efficiency, transparency, and coordination needed to address global issues in a structured and organized manner.

7.5. Statements Made in Plenary or Before a Main Committee

In plenary meetings or before a Main Committee in multilateral meetings, the statements made are significant and are often awaited with great attention. These declarations allow representatives of Member States to share their positions, present their policies, and express their concerns on issues of global interest.

7.5.1. Interpretation of Interventions[11]

According to the *Handbook for United Nations Delegations*, statements made at meetings with interpretation are interpreted into the other official languages of the UN. Speakers are encouraged to speak at a reasonable pace to enable the interpreters to render the statements accurately and completely. When speakers speak quickly to meet their speaking time, the quality of interpretation can suffer. It is recommended that you do not exceed a rate of 100 to 120 words per minute in

---

[11.] Guide for delegations (44).

English. It is not uncommon for some presiding officers to stop certain speakers and ask them to reduce the rate of their voices to facilitate the work of the translators.

If a statement is delivered in a language other than the official languages, the delegation concerned must provide interpretation or the text of the statement in one of the official languages. UN interpreters use this interpretation or translation, which is considered the official text of the declaration, to provide interpretation into the other official languages. The delegation must also provide a "pointer," a person who is proficient in both the original language of the statement and the official language into which it was translated, to guide the UN interpreter and ensure synchronization between the speaker and the interpreter. Specific arrangements for interpretation from non-official languages and access to interpretation booths for external interpreters at the UN should be agreed in advance with the Meetings Management Section.

Interpretation plays a crucial role in multilateral meetings by allowing communication between delegates who speak in different languages. Here are some important points to consider about interpreting at these events:

7.5.1.1. Simultaneous Interpretation

Simultaneous interpretation is the most common method of interpretation used at multilateral meetings. It involves interpreters working in soundproof booths and interpreting speakers' speeches in real time in the different working languages of the organization, usually the official languages of the UN. Participants can listen to the interpretations via headsets and select the language of their choice.

7.5.1.2. Consecutive Interpreting

Consecutive interpreting is another method used, although less frequent. In this case, the speaker speaks for a short period and then pauses to allow the interpreter to translate his or her speech into another language.[12] This slows down the flow of meetings and is typically used when the number of speakers is limited or when simultaneous interpretation resources are not available.

---

[12] *The Use of Pauses in Speeches*: Strategic pauses can enhance the impact of a speech. For example, Barack Obama is known for his calculated silences that amplify the power of his message.

7.5.2. Team of Interpreters

Interpreting at multilateral meetings is provided by teams of highly qualified interpreters. These interpreters are trained to work in specific fields such as diplomacy, politics, and economics to ensure accurate understanding and accurate translation of the speeches delivered. Teams of interpreters typically take turns every twenty to thirty minutes to ensure consistent quality and accuracy.

View of the Translator's Dressing Room During the Meeting to Present the Report of the International Court of Justice 2024

7.5.3. Challenges of Interpretation

Simultaneous interpreting presents unique challenges, including the need to stay focused for long periods, manage stress, and maintain an attentive listen. Interpreters must also be able to adapt quickly to different speech styles, understand complex concepts, and convey the cultural and linguistic nuances of speakers.

7.5.4. Role of Delegates

Delegates should be aware of the importance of interpretation and show respect for interpreters by speaking clearly, using understandable language, and avoiding overly long or complex sentences. They should also avoid speaking too quickly, which could make the interpreters' job more difficult.

7.5.5. Use of Written Documents

When written documents, such as statements, are distributed to delegates, it is recommended that they be provided in multiple languages to facilitate understanding and allow interpreters to consult them for more accurate translation.

In summary, interpretation plays a vital role in multilateral meetings by allowing for smooth and efficient communication between delegates of different languages. It requires professional interpreters, rigorous coordination, and cooperation between all participants to ensure fruitful exchanges and mutual understanding.

7.5.6. Written Translations of Statements Delivered in the Official Languages

When a delegation provides a written translation of its statement in the official languages, it must indicate on the first page of the text whether it is "to be read as is" or "to be checked at delivery." In the case of translations into more than one official language, the delegation should clearly state which of these translations should be considered as the official translation. This practice ensures the clarity and accuracy of statements made at multilateral meetings, ensuring that written materials accurately reflect what is said during interventions.

7.5.6.1. Reading the Text as Is

The interpreters will follow the translation provided. As a result, any changes, including omissions and additions, that the speaker might make to the text were unlikely to be reflected in the interpretation.

When statements are made in the official languages at multilateral meetings, it is essential to rely on official information provided by the UN to carry out written translations. Delegations should ensure that statements were properly translated into the other official languages of the Organization to facilitate understanding and communication among participants.

Written translations must be faithful to the speeches delivered, respecting the content, tone, and nuances expressed by the speakers. It is recommended that qualified professional translators with in-depth knowledge of the official languages and terminologies specific to the fields dealt with at multilateral meetings be used.

Official UN information, such as transcripts and audio recordings of statements, are reliable sources for written translations. It is important to refer to these sources to ensure the accuracy and authenticity of the translations.

Delegations should also ensure that written translations are available promptly, to allow participants to familiarize themselves with the statements in their own language and to better contribute to the discussions and negotiations.

In summary, when it comes to translating statements made into official languages at multilateral meetings, it is crucial to rely on official UN information to ensure accurate, reliable, and consistent written translations of the speeches delivered.

7.5.6.2. Reading with Verification at Pronouncement

The interpreters will follow the speaker and not the translation provided. If the speaker deviated from the text, the delegation should be aware that the interpretation heard in the Chamber would not necessarily correspond to the translation that it might have distributed to the audience and the press.

When statements are made in the official languages at multilateral meetings, it is essential to rely on official information provided by the UN to carry out written translations. Delegations should ensure that statements were properly translated into the other official languages of the Organization to facilitate understanding and communication among participants.

Written translations must be faithful to the speeches delivered, respecting the content, tone, and nuances expressed by the speakers. It is recommended that qualified professional translators with in-depth knowledge of the official languages and terminologies specific to the fields dealt with at multilateral meetings be used.

Official UN information, such as transcripts and audio recordings of statements, is a reliable source for written translations. It is important to refer to it in order to ensure the authenticity of the translations.

Delegations should also ensure that written translations were available in a timely manner, an order to allow participants to familiarize themselves with the statements in their own language and to better contribute to the discussions and negotiations.

In summary, when it comes to translating statements made into official languages at multilateral meetings, it is crucial to rely on official UN information to ensure accurate, reliable, and consistent written translations of the speeches delivered. This ensures smooth communication and mutual understanding between participants.

7.5.7. Microphones

The use of microphones in multilateral meetings is a key element in ensuring clear and effective communication. Microphones are typically activated when representatives are invited to speak, and they press the button corresponding to their microphone.

> In order for their speeches to be recorded and interpreted in the best possible way, speakers must speak directly and clearly in front of the microphone, especially when it comes to figures, quotes or very technical terms or when they read a speech written in advance. They are also asked to avoid tapping the microphone to check that it is working, turning pages, and making or taking calls on their mobile phones.

This system ensures that only authorized speakers speak and avoids interruptions or unwanted interventions. When a representative wants to speak, they should wait to be invited by the meeting chair or moderator, and then press their microphone button to unmute it.

This practice ensures order and organization in the exchanges, allowing each speaker to be clearly heard by all participants. In addition, it helps to avoid confusion and unwanted sound interference.

Representatives must follow the instructions for using microphones and wait their turn to speak. This helps to maintain a harmonious and equitable working environment, promoting the participation of all actors involved in the multilateral meeting.

In summary, microphones are activated when representatives are invited to speak and press the corresponding button. This practice ensures orderly communication and avoids unwanted interruptions, thus allowing for clear and effective exchanges at multilateral meetings.

7.5.8. Minutes and Minutes of Meetings

Written records are prepared for the plenary meetings of the main organs, the meetings of the Main Committees of the General Assembly and, on a limited and selective basis, the meetings of certain other organs. These may be either minutes of meetings or summary records. These documents are prepared by the Secretariat; Delegations may make corrections, but corrections that add to or modify the meaning of the speech delivered cannot be accepted.

- The minutes of the meeting report the debates in their entirety. They include a translation of the speeches delivered in the other languages as well as an edited transcript of the speeches delivered in the language used in the minutes.
- Delegations should be aware that any part of a written statement that is not read out at the meeting will not appear in the record of that meeting.
- The summary records report the proceedings in a concise and abbreviated form. They are not intended to systematically include each of the interventions or to reproduce them verbatim.
- The preparation of verbatim and summary records for UN organs is regulated by several decisions of the General Assembly or other principal organs.
- The "Overview" section of the *Journal* briefly presents the content of the session for reference.
- There are also audiovisual recordings of the debates of the sittings, which can be consulted (60).

Minutes and records of meetings play a critical role in multilateral meetings as they provide an accurate record of discussions, decisions made, and outcomes achieved. These documents serve as a reference for participants, delegations, and bodies responsible for the follow-up and implementation of the resolutions and commitments made at the meeting.

The minutes are official documents that record in detail the debates, the interventions of the participants, the decisions taken, the proposed amendments, and the results of the votes. They accurately reflect the proceedings of the meeting and serve as a basis for subsequent reports.

Minutes of meetings, on the other hand, are more concise documents that summarize the key points discussed at the meeting. They highlight key debates, decisions taken, and agreed actions. Minutes are often used for wider dissemination to interest parties or for external communication.

The preparation of minutes and minutes of meetings requires particular attention to the accuracy of information, clarity of wording, and neutrality in the presentation of facts. It is important to ensure a balanced representation of the views expressed and to avoid any interpretation or bias.

These documents are usually drafted by meeting secretaries or designated drafting teams, who are responsible for compiling interventions, decisions, and resolutions adopted. They rely on audio or video recordings of the meeting, transcripts of speeches, and notes taken during debates to ensure accurate transcription.

In conclusion, minutes and records of meetings are essential tools for documenting and reporting on discussions and decisions taken at multilateral meetings. They serve as a reference for monitoring and implementing the commitments made, as well as for communicating the results to the parties concerned.

7.5.8.1. Corrections to Be Made to Minutes of Meetings or Summary Records

- Please transmit any corrections to the minutes of the meeting to the Chief of the Verbatim Reporting Service (verbatim@un.org).
- Please transmit corrections to summary records to the Chief, Records Management Section (dms@un.org).
- Corrections must be made in accordance with what is indicated in the footnote on the first page of the minutes of meetings and summary records. If they are made on the text of a paper copy of the document to be corrected, the first page of the corrected document must bear the signature and title of an authorized member of the delegation concerned.
- Delegations are requested to ensure that corrections made by hand are legibly written and to indicate clearly where they are to be inserted.
- Corrections to the text of the minutes of the meeting shall relate only to errors[13] or omissions concerning statements actually made; they may relate only to the text of the language in which they were made. When a request for correction is submitted, a check is carried out by means of the audiovisual recording of the intervention in question.

[13.] A classic mistake is to adopt an overly aggressive tone. For example, Nikita Khrushchev's speech in 1960 at the UN, where he banged on his desk with his shoe, damaged the image of the USSR internationally.

7.5.8.2. Virtual or Hybrid Meetings Service

The Virtual or Hybrid Meetings Service offers a range of services and technology platforms designed to facilitate participation in virtual or hybrid meetings. These services include comprehensive support solutions for virtual meetings, best practices for effective use of these platforms, and advice on technology and bandwidth needs. Participants can receive assistance in planning and using these services, which may include training on virtual platform features, guidance on device configuration, and recommendations to ensure a stable internet connection. These services are available on demand to meet the specific needs of virtual or hybrid meeting organizers, providing a complete solution to facilitate remote participation and ensure virtual events run smoothly.

7.5.8.3. Pre-Recorded Speeches, Statements, Interventions, and Videos[14]

The Broadcasting and Conference Services Support Section facilitates the dissemination of pre-recorded speeches, statements, interventions, and videos at meetings as required. Information on the preferred file format, technological needs, and different means of submission as well as best practices is available upon request. Applications must be sent as soon as possible and no later than four working days before the meeting or event. The Broadcasting and Conference Services Support Section facilitates the provision of technologies and services to make meetings more accessible, such as permanent and on-demand captioning and the recording and broadcasting of sign language interpretation (email: request-for-services@un.org).

At multilateral meetings, it is common to use different formats of communication, such as speeches, statements, interventions, and pre-recorded videos. Each format offers specific benefits and meets the specific needs of meeting participants and organizers.

Speeches are usually delivered live by delegation representatives. They allow speakers to convey their messages in a clear and impactful way, providing detailed information on their country's positions, policies, or proposals. Speeches can be prepared in advance and read in front of the audience or delivered more spontaneously, depending on the format and standards of the meeting.

[14.] *Guide for Delegations*, 102.

Illustration of a Remote Intervention via Videoconference

Statements are like speeches, but they are often shorter and focus on specific points or topics. Statements may be made in response to other interventions, to express support or opposition to a proposal, or to share additional information.

The interventions are more informal speeches, often during group discussions or debates. Participants can share their views, ask questions, make observations, or make more interactive contributions. The interventions allow for active participation and promote the exchange of ideas between the participants.

Pre-recorded videos are increasingly being used in multilateral meetings. They offer flexibility in the presentation of content, allowing speakers to convey their messages in a more visual and creative way. Videos can include testimonials, feature stories, graphic presentations, or carefully prepared messages to engage and engage the audience.

Each communication format has its specific advantages. Speeches and statements allow speakers to present key information in a structured way, while interventions promote interactive exchanges and discussions. Pre-recorded videos offer creative opportunities to convey impactful messages and engage the audience in a visual way.

It is important to choose the most appropriate format based on the communication objectives, the target audience, and the context of the multilateral meeting. A judicious combination of these formats can contribute to effective communication and fruitful exchange between participants.

7.5.8.4. Retransmission, Streaming, and Audio Recordings

About the UN in particular, broadcasting, streaming, audio and video recording services are available for meetings and events. As access to recordings of closed meetings is restricted to the Chair and Secretary on duty during the meeting, requests for recordings of these meetings must be made by one of these persons. For virtual meetings and events, the Section provides interpretation platforms, broadcasting, webcasting, streaming, audio and video recording services. Applications must be sent as soon as possible and no later than four working days before the meeting or event.

At multilateral meetings, it is essential to provide means of broadcasting, streaming and audio recordings to ensure visibility, accessibility, and archiving of discussions and deliberations. These elements make it possible to reach a wider audience, promote transparency, and preserve a lasting record of events.

The broadcast consists of live broadcasting of the meetings of the multilateral meeting, thus allowing an external audience to follow the discussions in real time. This can be done through online platforms, specialty TV channels, webinars, or other suitable means of broadcasting. Live streaming expands the audience beyond the attendees in person and promotes audience participation and engagement.

Streaming, also known as streaming, allows participants to follow the meeting sessions live through a dedicated online platform. This provides the flexibility to connect remotely and follow the proceedings from any location with an internet connection. Streaming facilitates virtual participation and allows speakers and observers to stay informed and engaged throughout the meeting.

Audio recordings play a crucial role in archiving and preserving the discussions and decisions taken at the multilateral meeting. They capture the entire sittings, including speeches, debates, and votes. The audio recordings serve as a reference for the drafting of minutes, minutes of meetings, and subsequent reports. They also allow participants and interested parties to look back on past discussions and re-listen to key points discussed.

All of these retransmissions, streaming, and audio recording devices contribute to the transparency, accountability, and accessibility of multilateral meetings. They facilitate remote participation, information sharing, and dissemination of results to a wider audience. In addition, they allow for the creation of valuable archives for the preservation of the history and memory of multilateral meetings.

It is important to have an appropriate technical infrastructure and delivery protocols in place to ensure the quality and reliability of these devices. This includes the use of quality audiovisual equipment, a stable internet connection, reliable streaming platforms, and security measures to protect data and broadcast content.

In conclusion, broadcasting, streaming and audio recordings are essential elements in making multilateral meetings accessible, transparent, and sustainable. They allow remote participation, promote the dissemination of information, and ensure the preservation of the history of the proceedings.

7.5.8.5. Video Projections and Screens

The use of video projections and screens is common at multilateral meetings, especially at the UN, to facilitate visual communication and the presentation of visual content to participants. Video projections and screens provide additional visual support that enhances the impact of the messages and makes it easier to understand the information presented. Here are some things to consider about video projections and screens at these meetings.

7.5.8.6. Visual Presentation

Video projections are used to broadcast visual presentations such as slideshows, charts, videos, or infographics. This facilitates the communication of complex data, statistics, diagrams, or graphs that may be difficult to convey only orally. The screens allow a clear and crisp visualization of this content for all participants.

Visual Support for Speeches and Statements: Video projections can be used to accompany speeches and statements by speakers. Slides or videos can illustrate the key points discussed, provide concrete examples, or present images and videos that reinforce the message. This helps capture the audience's attention and improve information retention.

Viewing Documents and Resolutions: Screens can be used to display official documents such as resolutions, reports, or written statements. This allows participants to consult them simultaneously during discussions, promoting common understanding and informed decision-making.

Live Streaming and Recordings: Video projections can be used to live stream meeting sessions, allowing participants and the audience to follow the discussions remotely. In addition, video recordings can be made to archive the sessions and allow later consultation.

7.5.8.6.1. Interactive Technology

Interactive displays offer a range of features that can enrich multilateral meetings. By integrating interactive technologies such as touchscreens, organizers can boost attendee engagement and facilitate collaboration. For example, during discussions or negotiations, participants can use these screens to take notes in real time, annotate shared documents, or even vote electronically on outstanding issues. This approach promotes dynamic interaction and allows participants to actively contribute to the debates. Additionally, the use of interactive technology can increase the efficiency of meetings by allowing instant access to relevant information and facilitating decision-making. By integrating interactive technology into multilateral meetings, organizers can create more dynamic and collaborative work environments, thus promoting more efficient and productive exchanges between participants.

7.5.8.6.2. Technical Logistics

When planning multilateral meetings, it is important to provide an adequate technical infrastructure for video projections and screens. This includes choosing quality AV equipment, proper placement of screens in the room, proper cable, and connection management, as well as pre-testing to ensure that everything is working properly.

The use of video projections and screens in multilateral meetings contributes to effective visual communication, better understanding of information, and active participation of participants. It also helps to improve the impact of messages and facilitate informed decision-making.

7.5.8.6.3. Coordination with Other Delegations

In negotiations or coalitions, delegations may work with other countries to coordinate their statements. This may involve consultations, exchanges of notes, and harmonization of positions to present common messages at multilateral meetings.

It is important to note that practices may vary from one delegation to another and depend on the internal resources and procedures of each country. Some speakers may also receive advice or suggestions from political advisers or senior officials before finalizing their statements. Overall, the drafting of declarations is a complex process that requires a thorough understanding of the diplomatic issues, national policies, and objectives of each delegation. Speakers play a vital role in the preparation of their statements, whether they are directly involved in the drafting or collaborate with specialized teams within their delegation.

7.5.8.6.4. Remove Your Delegation's Name from the List of Authors

A representative should first inform the General Assembly Affairs Branch that his or her Mission intends to withdraw from the list of sponsors, by sending an email to the contacts listed here. It is no longer possible to remove oneself from the list of sponsors after the resolution has been adopted.

Overall Conclusion

This in-depth exploration of multilateral meetings and the issues related to speaking and speechwriting in these complex contexts offers a comprehensive understanding of contemporary diplomatic dynamics. Through the different sections of this guide, we have covered a variety of topics, ranging from the importance of multilateral meetings to managing the specific challenges faced at these events.

In concluding this book, a retrospective look at the rich fabric of multilateral meetings reveals a complex web of diplomatic interactions. Every word spoken, every statement made, contributes to the construction of the global architecture of international relations. Through these pages, we have embarked on a journey into the very essence of multilateral diplomacy, exploring the intricacies of speaking out and the mysteries of negotiations on a global scale.

This guide, forged in the crucible of the UN and international forums, serves not only as a practical compendium but also as an invitation to reflection. Multilateral meetings, as a melting pot where collective destinies are forged, require constant mastery of diplomatic codes. Every statement made is an essential piece in the puzzle of global diplomacy, and this guide is an indispensable companion for those who aspire to excel in this delicate art.

The crucial importance of these meetings transcends national borders, calling for a deep understanding of contemporary geopolitical issues. Through a rigorous methodology, combining diplomatic experience with academic research, we sought to provide readers with a robust tool adapted to the complex challenges of international diplomacy.

Indeed, whether you are a seasoned diplomat, a political representative, or a civil society actor, mastery of speaking at multilateral meetings remains an imperative skill. UN meetings, international summits, and thematic conferences are all stages where *The Diplomatic Voice* makes itself heard, influencing the course of world events.

The challenges are many, from language barriers to differences of opinion, but through these pages, we have sought to arm the reader with the tools necessary to navigate these often-tumultuous diplomatic waters with confidence. The rigorous structure of this book, rooted in an in-depth contextual analysis, a comprehensive literature review, and practical examples from real-life multilateral meetings, aims to provide a comprehensive resource.

On a personal level, writing this guide has been an exciting and rewarding undertaking. My own experience as minister counselor at the Permanent Mission of Haiti to the UN has informed my understanding of the nuances of multilateral diplomacy. As an active delegate to the Sixth Committee of the UN General Assembly, I have had the privilege of participating in complex negotiations, bringing a practical perspective to this book.

As you read these pages, I invite you to consider speaking in multilateral meetings as an art in constant evolution. May this book serve as a compass in your diplomatic journeys, offering practical advice, rich perspectives, and continued inspiration to make every statement a meaningful contribution to the world stage. May you, as a reader, find in these lines valuable resources to refine your diplomatic pen and make your voice heard with confidence and conviction in the corridors of multilateral diplomacy.

In conclusion, *The Diplomatic Voice* stands as a comprehensive guide, offering an in-depth dive into the complex art of diplomatic communication at multilateral meetings. Through these pages, readers explored the nuances of speaking out in crucial international forums, learning how to make impactful statements, influence debates, and forge meaningful alliances.

The book has traced a solid methodological path, combining diplomatic experience, in-depth research, and expertise in public communication. Practical advice was supported by concrete examples from real-life multilateral meetings, providing readers with a tangible perspective on the application of the principles discussed.

Each chapter helped to demystify the mysteries of the different facets of multilateral diplomacy, whether it was the careful preparation of declarations, the management of the various meeting formats, or the navigation of the challenges inherent in international negotiations.

The importance of multilateral meetings as essential pivots in global diplomacy was clearly emphasized, as was the crucial role of declarations as powerful instruments in formulating policies, building alliances, and solving global problems.

By providing rich perspectives, sound advice, and innovative solutions, *The Diplomatic Voice* aspires to be an indispensable companion for anyone who aspires to excel in the complex world of multilateral meetings. Whether influencing global policy, promoting peace, or resolving humanitarian crises, this guide offers practical tools to make one's voice heard with confidence and conviction.

As the world continues to evolve on the international stage, this book encourages readers to stay informed of recent developments, highlighting the need for constant adaptation to succeed in the dynamic field of multilateral diplomacy.

The Diplomatic Voice stands as a valuable resource, intended to equip diplomats, students, researchers, and all those engaged in international affairs with the skills to successfully navigate through multilateral for a and contribute significantly to building a world of progress, mutual understanding, and world peace.

In conclusion, this guide is not only intended to be a theoretical exploration but a practical tool for those who engage in multilateral meetings. Prospects could include continuous adaptation to changes in the diplomatic landscape, continuous training for key actors, and increased awareness of the importance of multilateral communication.

Finally, the wealth of information contained in this guide provides a solid foundation for those seeking to excel in the delicate art of speaking and speechwriting in multilateral meetings. Modern diplomacy requires skillful and nuanced communication, and this guide aspires to be a reliable companion for those embracing this challenge. May these pages stimulate reflection, inspire action, and contribute to more effective and fruitful diplomatic exchanges in the future.

REFERENCES

Ambrosetti, David. 2009. *Normes et rivalités diplomatiques à l'ONU: le Conseil de sécurité en audience*. Regards sur l'international 8. P.I.E. Peter Lang.

———. 2013. "Les négociations diplomatiques au Conseil de sécurité." In *Négociations internationales*. Presses de Sciences Po, pp. 235–259.

Archambault-Küch, Marie-Laure. 2022. "Les stratégies vestimentaires des membres des délégations hedjazienne, syrienne et libanaise à la Conférence de la Paix de Paris, 1919." *Histoire, Europe et relations internationales* 1 (1): 123–135. https://doi.org/10.3917/heri.001.0123.

archivesRC, réal. 2020. *Le 24 juillet 1967, le général de Gaulle en discours à Montréal déclare "Vive le Québec libre!*." https://www.youtube.com/watch?v=amApwFT49JQ.

Arifon, Olivier. 2010. "Langue diplomatique et langage formel: un code à double entente." *Hermès, La Revue* 58 (3): 69–78. https://doi.org/10.3917/herm.058.0069.

Assemblée générale des Nations Unies. 2013. "Malala Yousafzai devant l'Assemblée des Nations Unies pour la Jeunesse." *Office of the Secretary-General's Envoy on Youth* (blog). https://www.un.org/youthenvoy/fr/video/malala-yousafzai-devant-lassemblee-nations-unies-jeunesse/.

Avenier, Marie-josé. 2011. "Les paradigmes épistémologiques constructivistes : post-modernisme ou pragmatisme ?" *Management & Avenir* 43: 372–391. https://doi.org/10.3917/mav.043.0372.

Balzacq, Thierry, and Frédéric Ramel. 2013. *Traité de relations internationales*. Sciences po, les presses.

Bettati, Mario. 2012. *Le Droit international de l'environnement*. Odile Jacob.

Bounding, Kenneth E. 1968. "Book Review: David Easton. *A Systems Analysis of Political Life*. New York: John Wiley, 1965." *Behavioral Science* 13 (2): 147–149. https://doi.org/10.1002/bs.3830130208.

Cresswell, Robert. 1968. "Le Geste Manuel Associé Au Langage." *Langages* 10: 119–127. https://www.jstor.org/stable/41680681.

Crozier, Michel, and Erhard Friedberg. 1996. *L'acteur et le systéme: les contraintes de l'action collective.* Collection Points Série Essais 248. Éd. du Seuil.

———. 2014. *L'acteur et le système les contraintes de l'action collective.* Éd. du Seuil.

Crozier, Michel, and Jean-Claude Thoenig. 1975. "La régulation des systèmes organisés complexes: Le cas du système de décision politico-administratif local en France." *Revue Française de Sociologie* 16 (1): 3. https://doi.org/10.2307/3321128.

Delporte, Christian. 2009. *Histoire de la communication politique en France.* Paris: Presses Universitaires de France.

Donahue, Ray T., and Michael H. Prosser. 1997. *Diplomatic Discourse: International Conflict at the United Nations.* Bloomsbury Academic.

Fleury, Antoine, and Georges-Henri Soutou. 2005. "Les nouveaux outils de la diplomatie au XXe siècle." *Relations internationales* 121 (1): 3–7. https://doi.org /10.3917/ri.121.0003.

Friedberg, Erhard. 2009. "Pouvoir et négociation." *Négociations* 12 (2): 15–22. https://doi.org/10.3917/neg.012.0015.

Gaspard, Fritzner. 2012. "Guide d'interventions à l'usage des délégué haïtiens." Haitian Ministry of Foreign Affairs.

Gauthier, Gilles. 2005. "Le constructivisme." *Questions de communication* 7: 121–146. http://questionsdecommunication.revues.org/4625.

Jollet, Anne. 2012. "Review of *Review of Paroles de négociateurs. L'entretien dans la pratique diplomatique de la fin du Moyen Âge à la fin du XIX e siècle,* par Stefano Andretta, Stéphane Péquignot, Marie-Karine Schaub, Jean-Claude Waquet, et Christian Windler." *Annales historiques de la Révolution française* 370: 268–271. https://www.jstor.org/stable/41890814.

Kissinger, Henry A. 1956. "Reflections on American diplomacy." *Foreign Affairs* 35 (1): 37–56. https://doi.org/10.2307/20031204.

Kissinger, Henry. 2014. "Diplomacy." In *Geopolitics.* Routledge (pp. 114–115).

Kristeva, Julia. 1968. "Le Geste, Pratique Ou Communication ?" *Langages* 10: 48–64. https://www.jstor.org/stable/41680674.

Kurbalija, Jovan, and Hannah Slavik. 2001. *Language and Diplomacy*. Diplo Foundation.

Lagadec, Patrick. 2012. "Gestion de crise: nouvelle donne." *Sécurité et stratégie* 10 (3): 50–52. https://doi.org/10.3917/sestr.010.0050.

Leloir, Louis. 1886. *L'art de dire: Extraits commentés de Molière, Corneille, Racine et La Fontaine*. H. Lecène et H. Oudin.

Lequesne, Christian. 2021. *La puissance par l'image: les États et leur diplomatie publique*. L'enjeu mondial. SciencesPo les presses.

Lévy, Philippe. 1984. "La diplomatie multilatérale au niveau mondial : les aléas des négociations onusiennes sur les codes de conduite en matière de sociétés transnationales et de transfert de technologie." *Relations internationales* 40: 475–481. https://www.jstor.org/stable/45342316.

Liu, Shuang, Zala Volcic, and Cindy Gallois. 2010. *Introducing Intercultural Communication: Global Cultures and Contexts*. SAGE.

Lurçat, Liliane. 1973. "Du geste au langage." *Bulletin de psychologie* 26 (304): 501–505. https://doi.org/10.3406/bupsy.1973.10409.

Lynch, C. M., and A. Klotz. 1999. "Le Constructivisme Dans La Théorie Des Relations Internationales." *Critique Internationale* 2 (2): 51–62. https://escholarship.org/uc/item/4c07m601.

Maurice, Antoine. 2002. "La diplomatie multilatérale entre babil et Babel." *Dans Les mots du pouvoir*, édité par Gilbert Rist. Graduate Institute Publications. https://doi.org/10.4000/books.iheid.2465.

Mérimée-Dufourcq, Marguerite. 1995. "Les représentations permanentes auprès de l'Union Européenne." These de doctorat, Paris 1.

Mulholland, Joan. 1991. *The Language of Negotiation: A Handbook of Practical Strategies for Improving Communication*. Routledge.

Nations Unies. 2018. "L'Iran fustige à l'ONU la politique américaine de l'administration Trump—ONU Info." September 25, 2018. https://news.un.org/fr/story/2018/09/1024572.

———. 2022. "Budget de l'ONU 2022—wisnique.panier@diplomatie.ht—Messagerie Diplomatie.ht." 2022. https://mail.google.com/mail/u/0/#inbox/FMfcgzGwJmNbGTQGBwLdnXzkVFlXwxvW?projector=1&messagePartId=0.1.

———. 2023. "Fonctionnement de l'Assemblée générale des Nations Unies." Nations Unies. August 11, 2023. https://www.un.org/fr/ga/about/background.shtml.

———. 2024. "About Us FR—Nations Unies." United Nations, January 22, 2024. https://www.un.org/fr/about-us.

O'Hara, Kenton P., Michael Massimi, Richard Harper, Simon Rubens, and Jessica Morris. 2014. "Everyday Dwelling with WhatsApp." In *Proceedings of the 17th ACM Conference on Computer Supported Cooperative Work & Social Computing*. CSCW '14, 1131-43. https://doi.org/10.1145/2531602.2531679

Panier, Wisnique. 2014. *Zo Kiki : Un phénomène à comprendre pour agir.* Édilivre.

Porter, Michael E. 2024. "Michael Porter on Competition—Michael E. Porter, 1999." s. d. Consulté le, January 23, 2024. *Antitrust Bulletin* 44 (4): 841–880. https://journals.sagepub.com/doi/abs/10.1177/0003603X9904400405?journalCode=abxa.

Postel-Vinay, Karoline, Michel Bruneau, Jean-Marc Sorel, Béatrice Giblin, Christian Grataloup, Jean-François Staszak, Olivier Kramsch, Frédéric Ramel, Yann Richard, Frédéric Charillon, and Jean-Paul Chagnollaud. 2013. *La frontière ou l'invention des relations internationales, phénomène diasporique, transnationalisme, lieux et territoires, la frontière comme enjeu de droit international, frontières, territoire, sécurité, souveraineté.* CERISCOPE.

Reith, Sally. 2010. "Money, Power, and Donor–NGO Partnerships." *Development in Practice* 20 (3): 446–455. https://doi.org/10.1080/09614521003709932.

Revel, Claude. 2011. "Diplomatie économique multilatérale et influence." *Géoéconomie* 56 (1): 59–67. https://doi.org/10.3917/geoec.056.0059.

Rigal-Cellard, Bernadette. 2003. "Le président Bush et la rhétorique de l'axe du mal. Droite chrétienne, millénarisme et messianisme américain." *Études* 399 (9): 153–162.

Ringe, Nils. 2022. *The Language(s) of Politics: Multilingual Policy-Making in the European Union.* University of Michigan Press.

Schulzinger, Robert D. 2019. *"Henry Kissinger: Doctor of Diplomacy."* Columbia University Press.

Smouts, Marie-Claude. 1991. "L'Afrique dans la diplomatie multilatérale." *Études internationales* 22 (2): 267–278. https://doi.org/10.7202/702838ar.

Tchemako, Olivia De Mattei. 2018. "Discours aux Nations Unies : des normes pour un genre 'poli' ?" *Corela. Cognition, représentation, langage* 16 (2): 1–18. https://doi.org/10.4000/corela.6956.

Telbami, S. 2002. "Kenneth Waltz, Neorealism, and Foreign Policy." *Security Studies* 11 (3): 158–170. https://doi.org/10.1080/714005344.

Tremblay, Jean-Marie. 2005. "Constanze VILLAR, Le discours diplomatique." In le discours diplomatique, edited by Constanze Villar. L'Harmattan. http://classiques.uqac.ca/contemporains/villar_constanze/discours_diplomatique/discours_diplomatique_intro.html

UN Office of Public Information. 1961. *How to Plan and Conduct Model U.N. Meetings: A Handbook for Organizers*. Oceana Library on the United Nations. Oceana Publications.

Villar, Constanze. 2006a. *Le discours diplomatique*. Pouvoirs comparés. L'Harmattan.

———. 2006b. *Le discours diplomatique*. Editions L'Harmattan.

von Bertalanffy, Ludwig, and Jean B. Chabrol. 1980. *Théorie générale des systèmes*. Dunod.

Waltz, Kenneth N. 2014. "Realist thought and neorealist theory." In *The Realism Reader*. Routledge.

Waswo, Richard. 2011. "Le Style des gestes: Corporéité et kinésie dans le récit littéraire." *Poetics Today* 32 (2): 391–392. https://doi.org/10.1215/03335372-1162722.